Foucault: A Very Short Introduction

VERY SHORT INTRODUCTIONS are for anyone wanting a stimulating and accessible way into a new subject. They are written by experts, and have been translated into more than 45 different languages.

The series began in 1995, and now covers a wide variety of topics in every discipline. The VSI library currently contains over 600 volumes—a Very Short Introduction to everything from Psychology and Philosophy of Science to American History and Relativity—and continues to grow in every subject area.

Very Short Introductions available now:

ABOLITIONISM Richard S. Newman
ACCOUNTING Christopher Nobes
ADAM SMITH Christopher J. Berry
ADOLESCENCE Peter K. Smith
ADVERTISING Winston Fletcher
AFRICAN AMERICAN
    RELIGION Eddie S. Glaude Jr
AFRICAN HISTORY John Parker and
    Richard Rathbone
AFRICAN POLITICS Ian Taylor
AFRICAN RELIGIONS
    Jacob K. Olupona
AGEING Nancy A. Pachana
AGNOSTICISM Robin Le Poidevin
AGRICULTURE Paul Brassley and
    Richard Soffe
ALEXANDER THE GREAT
    Hugh Bowden
ALGEBRA Peter M. Higgins
AMERICAN CULTURAL
    HISTORY Eric Avila
AMERICAN FOREIGN
    RELATIONS Andrew Preston
AMERICAN HISTORY Paul S. Boyer
AMERICAN IMMIGRATION
    David A. Gerber
AMERICAN LEGAL
    HISTORY G. Edward White
AMERICAN NAVAL
    HISTORY Craig L. Symonds
AMERICAN POLITICAL
    HISTORY Donald Critchlow
AMERICAN POLITICAL PARTIES
    AND ELECTIONS L. Sandy Maisel

AMERICAN POLITICS
    Richard M. Valelly
THE AMERICAN
    PRESIDENCY Charles O. Jones
THE AMERICAN
    REVOLUTION Robert J. Allison
AMERICAN SLAVERY
    Heather Andrea Williams
THE AMERICAN WEST Stephen Aron
AMERICAN WOMEN'S
    HISTORY Susan Ware
ANAESTHESIA Aidan O'Donnell
ANALYTIC PHILOSOPHY
    Michael Beaney
ANARCHISM Colin Ward
ANCIENT ASSYRIA Karen Radner
ANCIENT EGYPT Ian Shaw
ANCIENT EGYPTIAN ART AND
    ARCHITECTURE Christina Riggs
ANCIENT GREECE Paul Cartledge
THE ANCIENT NEAR EAST
    Amanda H. Podany
ANCIENT PHILOSOPHY Julia Annas
ANCIENT WARFARE Harry Sidebottom
ANGELS David Albert Jones
ANGLICANISM Mark Chapman
THE ANGLO-SAXON AGE John Blair
ANIMAL BEHAVIOUR
    Tristram D. Wyatt
THE ANIMAL KINGDOM
    Peter Holland
ANIMAL RIGHTS David DeGrazia
THE ANTARCTIC Klaus Dodds
ANTHROPOCENE Erle C. Ellis

Available soon:

For more information visit our website

www.oup.com/vsi/

Gary Gutting

FOUCAULT

A Very Short Introduction

SECOND EDITION

OXFORD
UNIVERSITY PRESS

OXFORD

UNIVERSITY PRESS

Great Clarendon Street, Oxford, OX2 6DP,
United Kingdom

Oxford University Press is a department of the University of Oxford.
It furthers the University's objective of excellence in research, scholarship,
and education by publishing worldwide. Oxford is a registered trade mark of
Oxford University Press in the UK and in certain other countries

© Gary Gutting 2005

The moral rights of the author have been asserted

First edition published 2005
Second edition published 2019

Impression: 3

Published in the United States of America by Oxford University Press
198 Madison Avenue, New York, NY 10016, United States of America

British Library Cataloguing in Publication Data

Data available

Library of Congress Control Number: 2019945038

ISBN 978-0-19-883078-8

Printed in Great Britain by
Ashford Colour Press Ltd, Gosport, Hampshire

To Anastasia
as always
with love

Contents

Author's note to the second edition

I've added a new chapter (Chapter 11, 'Foucault after Foucault') on material published after Foucault's death, especially the Collège de France lectures and *Confessions of the Flesh*, the fourth volume of the *History of Sexuality*. There are also some corresponding modifications to Chapter 10, and a few revisions in other chapters.

Thanks to OUP's Andrea Keegan (who suggested this new edition) and Jenny Nugee for their support. And special thanks, once again, to Anastasia Friel Gutting, the first and best reader of all my work.

Acknowledgements
for the first edition

I wrote the first draft of this essay during summer 2003, in conjunction with my seminar on Foucault at the Johann Wolfgang Goethe Universität in Frankfurt. Many thanks to Axel Honneth for his invitation and many kindnesses, to the students in my Foucault seminar for their interest and questions, and to the staff at the Literaturhaus Restaurant (especially Oliver and Franz) for their hospitality, good food, and splendid wine.

As always, the first and best reader of my manuscript was my wife, Anastasia Friel Gutting. I am also grateful for very helpful comments from Jerry Bruns and Todd May. My thanks to Marsha Filion of OUP for suggesting and supporting this project.

List of illustrations

The publisher and the author apologize for any errors or omissions in the above list. If contacted they will be pleased to rectify these at the earliest opportunity.

Abbreviations

The following abbreviations are used throughout to denote works by Foucault.

Foucault's books

AK (DL)   *The Archaeology of Knowledge*, tr. Alan Sheridan (New York: Vintage, 1972). Also includes 'The Discourse on Language' (DL), a translation of *L'ordre du discours*, Foucault's inaugural address at the Collège de France.

BC   *The Birth of the Clinic*, tr. Alan Sheridan (New York: Vintage, 1973).

CF   *Confessions of the Flesh*, Volume 4 of *The History of Sexuality* [to come]

CS   *The Care of the Self*, Volume 3 of *The History of Sexuality*, tr. Robert Hurley (New York: Vintage, 1986).

DP   *Discipline and Punish*, tr. Alan Sheridan (New York: Vintage, 1977).

HF   *Histoire de la folie à l'âge classique* (Paris: Gallimard, 1972).

HS   *The History of Sexuality*, Volume 1: *An Introduction*, tr. Robert Hurley (New York: Vintage, 1978).

MC	*Madness and Civilization*, tr. Richard Howard (New York: Vintage, 1965). This is a greatly abridged translation of HF.
OT	*The Order of Things*, tr. Alan Sheridan (New York: Vintage, 1970). Translation of *Les mots et les choses*.
RR	*Death and the Labyrinth: The World of Raymond Roussel*, tr. Charles Ruas (Garden City, NY: Doubleday and Co., 1986). Translation of *Raymond Roussel*. Includes an interview of Foucault by Charles Ruas.
UP	*The Use of Pleasures*, Volume 2 of *The History of Sexuality*, tr. Robert Hurley (New York: Vintage, 1985).

Collections of Foucault's articles, lectures, and interviews

DE	Daniel Defert and François Ewald (eds), *Dits et écrits, 1954–1988*, four volumes (Paris: Gallimard, 1994). Includes virtually everything, other than his books, that Foucault published.
EW	*The Essential Works of Michel Foucault*, ed. Paul Rabinow. A three-volume translation of selections from *Dits et écrits*.
EW I	Volume 1, *Ethics: Subjectivity and Truth*, ed. Paul Rabinow, tr. Robert Hurley et al. (New York: New Press, 1997).
EW II	Volume 2, *Aesthetics: Method and Epistemology*, ed. James Faubion, tr. Robert Hurley et al. (New York: New Press, 1998).
EW III	Volume 3, *Power*, ed. James Faubion, tr. Robert Hurley et al. (New York: New Press, 2000).
P/K	Colin Gordon (ed.), *Power/Knowledge: Selected Interviews and Other Writings, 1972–1977* (New York: Pantheon, 1980).

Foucault

PPC   Lawrence Kritzman (ed.), *Michel Foucault:*
Philosophy, Politics, Culture, tr. Alan Sheridan
(London: Routledge, 1988).

These last two collections contain some important pieces not in EW.

Collège de France lectures

English translations of the thirteen volumes of the lectures have
been published by Palgrave Macmillan, under the general
editorship of Arnold I. Davidson. Titles (and years the lectures
were delivered) are given in Chapter 11.

Chapter 1
Lives and works

I give Foucault (Figure 1) the first word: 'Do not ask who I am and do not ask me to remain the same... Let us leave it to our bureaucrats and our police to see that our papers are in order' (AK, 17).

He has his wish, since quite different readings of his life are supported by the known facts. One version of his story is a standard one of progressive academic success:

The son of a prominent provincial family, his father a successful doctor, Paul-Michel Foucault was a brilliant student, a star even, at the prestigious École Normale Supérieure. His academic and political connections enabled him to avoid the high-school teaching usually expected in France of those with philosophical academic ambitions. Instead, he spent several *Wanderjahren* in Sweden, Poland, and Germany, while finishing his dissertation, which was sponsored by one of the most powerful professors at the Sorbonne and, once published, gained favourable reviews from leading intellectuals. In the course of the next eight years he moved easily through a series of professorships. His 1966 book, *Les mots et les choses*, was an academic bestseller that made him the leading candidate to succeed Sartre as the French 'master-thinker'. A few years later, he won election to the super-elite Collège de France (following Bergson and Merleau-Ponty), which put him at the

1. **Foucault at the top of his class, Poitiers, 1944.**

pinnacle of the French academic world and relieved him of
ordinary teaching obligations. From then on, he travelled the world
(to Japan, Brazil, California, among other countries) lecturing to
packed halls, increasingly engaged in high-profile political actions,
and still managing to write brilliant books on crime and sex that

2

have made him a major figure in every humanistic and social scientific discipline. By the time he died, in 1984, he had already been the subject of dozens of books, and his posthumous fame has only increased.

But there is another, equally plausible version:

Foucault was a brilliant but emotionally troubled son of an authoritarian physician. A tormented homosexual, he may have attempted suicide while at the École Normale and was certainly under psychiatric care. He so hated French society that he fled to a series of marginal posts in foreign countries, where, however, he failed to find the liberation he sought. Despite spectacular intellectual success, he spent his life seeking extreme sensations ('limit-experiences', as he called them) from drugs and sadomasochistic sex, and died before he was 60 from AIDS, probably contracted at San Francisco bathhouses.

We can also tell the story of his life as one of political and social commitment and activism:

Foucault was fiercely independent and committed from the beginning to his own and others' freedom. His hatred of oppression flared out in the midst of the most complex and erudite discussions. He saw even his most esoteric intellectual work as contributing to a 'toolbox' for those opposing various tyrannies. And he had the effect he desired: he was a hero of the anti-psychiatry movement, of prison reform, of gay liberation…

None of these stories is false, but their mutual truth keeps us from forming any definitive picture of Foucault's life, which is just what he wanted. There's an underlying wisdom in such titles as *Hallucinating Foucault* (a novel by Patricia Duncker) and 'Foucault as I Imagine Him' (an obituary by Maurice Blanchot). At least for the present, we know too little about Foucault's personal life to do anything more than speculate about its relation

ma photo à 18 ans
Raymond Roussel
, Mai 1933

2. Raymond Roussel aged 18, 1895.

to his work. James Miller's *The Passions of Michel Foucault* shows both the limited possibilities and the distinct dangers of such speculation.

But why insist on reading the life into the work when the life can be read out of the work? Much of Foucault's existence was the writing of his books, and these tell us more about him than can the set of random anecdotes that have escaped the distortions of memories and Foucault's own efforts to maintain a private life.

The best starting point is *Raymond Roussel*, Foucault's only book-length literary study, and a work that he characterized as 'something very personal' (RR, interview, 185). Foucault's very choice of Roussel (Figure 2) as a subject is revelatory. Roussel (1877–1933) was, even as late as the 1950s, when Foucault first stumbled on his work in a Left Bank bookstore, a neglected and marginal writer, an 'experimentalist', but one who wrote not out of any literary theory or movement but from a megalomaniac sense of his own importance as a writer. (Indeed, Roussel was examined by Pierre Janet, the famous psychiatrist, who diagnosed him as suffering from a 'transformed religious mania'.) Inherited wealth allowed Roussel to devote all his time to writing, but the poems, plays, and novels he produced from 1894 until his death were, apart from some patronizing interest from the surrealists and genuine admiration from the novelist Raymond Queneau, greeted with derision or indifference.

This was hardly surprising, since Roussel's works were oddities even by the standards of the avant-garde, characterized by minute descriptions of objects and actions and often written, as he explained in his essay (by his instruction published only posthumously), 'How I Wrote Certain of My Books', according to his own bizarre formal rules of construction. He would, for example, require himself to begin and end a story with phrases that differed from one another in only one letter but had entirely different meanings. So, one story begins 'Les lettres du blanc sur les bandes du vieux billard' ('The white letters on the cushions of the old billiard table') and ends with 'les lettres du blanc sur les bandes du vieux pillard' ('the white man's letters about the hordes of the old plunderer'). Roussel also employed numerous other constraints based on double meanings of homonymic expressions.

Foucault was attracted, first of all, by Roussel's very marginality—his lack of literary success and classification as 'mentally ill'. He always had an interest in and sympathy for those excluded by mainstream standards. This may have initially been little more than the characteristic French intellectual's horror of the bourgeoisie, but it developed into a strong personal commitment to oppose the normative exclusions that define our society. From this commitment derived both Foucault's eventual social activism (for example, his work for prison reform) and his conception of his writings as a 'toolbox' to be utilized by those struggling for social and political transformation.

But Foucault was also fascinated by Roussel's exclusion of human subjectivity. This exclusion is signalled first by the dominance in Roussel's writings of spatial objectivity over temporal subjectivity. He typically offers elaborate descriptions of objects or actions, not narratives of characters and their experiences. Nor, on another level, are the works expressions of the author's subjectivity. Because of the strong subordination to formal rules, the words written flow more from the impersonal structures of language itself than from Roussel's thoughts and feelings. Foucault's interest in this sort of writing corresponds to his declaration that he himself 'writes in order to have no face' (AK, 17), to lose any fixed identity in the succession of masks he assumes in his books. As he said not long before his death: 'The main interest in life and work is to become someone else that you were not in the beginning' ('Truth, Power, Self', 9).

Foucault explicitly connects this loss of self in language with the absolute limit and abolition of subjectivity—death. His analysis of Roussel's works gives a central place to the author's obscure and ambiguous death: he was found on the floor of his hotel room in front of a locked door (always before kept open), which he may have been trying to open to save himself, or which he may have locked to keep himself from being saved. For Foucault, the situation of this death corresponds to the 'key' to his writings Roussel offers in 'How I Wrote Certain of My Books': just as we cannot know whether he wanted to use the key to his door to let others in or to keep them out, so we cannot know whether the literary key is meant to open up or close off the meaning of his texts. And it is his death that prevents us from resolving either question. Further, the death that prevents us from assessing the value of Roussel's literary key itself corresponds to the language of his books, which, as we have seen, has systematically suppressed the subjective life of both the author and his characters.

6

We have no way of knowing whether this focus on death—which continues throughout Foucault's writings—led, as Miller encourages us to speculate, to Foucault's deliberately putting himself and others at risk from AIDS. But there is no doubt that his work shows a fascination with the loss of self brought both by death and by its mirror in the linguistic formalism of writing such as Roussel's.

Commentators have generally left *Raymond Roussel* outside the canon of Foucault's major works, no doubt for the plausible reason that it is not, like the rest, a history. Foucault himself was content with this omission: 'I would go so far as to say that [*Raymond Roussel*] doesn't have a place in the sequence of my books...No one has paid much attention to this book, and I'm glad; it's my secret affair' (RR, interview, 185).

But, although the book does not fit into standard accounts of Foucault's projects of philosophically informed and oriented history, its preoccupations recur in his other books, particularly in *The Birth of the Clinic*, also published in 1963, which begins: 'This book is about space, about language, and about death' (BC, ix). Of course, in this study of the emergence of modern clinical medicine during the 19th century, these themes are significantly transposed. The 'space' is that of plague-infested cities, of hospital charity wards, of the sites of lesions in dissected cadavers; the language that of medical symptoms and probabilities; and death, of course, is the physical reality itself, not a symbol of marginalized subjectivity.

But as in Foucault's literary study, the concern with space (as opposed to time) and with language (as an autonomous system) reflects a mode of thought that removes subjectivity from its usual central position and subordinates it to structural systems. And death, in Foucault's history of modern medicine, remains at the heart of human existence. It is not mere extinction but 'a possibility intrinsic to life' (BC, 156), one that grounds

7

(through the dissections of pathological anatomy) our scientific knowledge of life. 'Death', Foucault concludes, 'left its old tragic heaven and became the lyrical core of man: his invisible truth, his visible secret' (BC, 172).

In many ways, *The Birth of the Clinic* is the scientific counterpart of the aestheticism of *Raymond Roussel*, exhibiting in the mode of close historical analysis the preoccupations that guided Foucault's patient exploration of Roussel's baroque complexifications. But one striking difference between the two books is *Raymond Roussel*'s lack of the flashes of savage critique that occasionally burst out of *The Birth of the Clinic*'s sustained erudition. For example, in the latter's Preface, after a preliminary sketch of the main stages of the discussion to come—and before some concluding comments about historical methodology—Foucault suddenly attacks the claim that modern medicine achieves 'the most concentrated formulation of an old medical humanism, as old as man's compassion' and denounces 'the mindless phenomenologies of understanding' that 'mingle the sand of their conceptual desert with this half-baked notion'.

He goes on to deride the 'feebly eroticized vocabulary...of the doctor/patient relationship [*le couple médicin—malade*]', which, he says, 'exhausts itself in trying to communicate the pale powers of matrimonial fantasies to so much non-thought' (BC, xiv). Such outbursts, even though occasional, are characteristic of Foucault's historical studies and signal, as we shall see, their ultimately political agenda. By contrast, *Raymond Roussel* shows a Foucault totally entranced in aesthetic enjoyment for its own sake, composing a memoir of the 'happy period' when Roussel 'was my love for several summers' (RR, interview, 185). This contrast is an early and striking instance of what I will argue is a fundamental tension in Foucault's life and thought between aesthetic contemplation and political activism.

Chapter 2
Literature

We have seen how Foucault wanted to write books in order to escape from any fixed identity, to continually become someone else, thereby never really being anyone. Eventually, we will have to ask why he would seek such a thing, but for now let's try to understand the project better.

A sceptical reader may suggest that Foucault's effort to escape identity through writing is an impossible project, since precisely by taking up a career of writing he achieved a quite definite and distinctive identity: that of an author. Indeed, isn't a famous and important author what Michel Foucault was and still is? Isn't this his identity?

Foucault's response to this objection will be the title of one of his best-known essays: 'What Is an Author?'. Is being an author a matter of having an identity (a certain nature, character, personality), like, for example, being a hero, a liar, or a lover? Does writing make me a certain kind of person?

Let's start with a common-sense definition of an author: someone who writes books. Or, to be a bit more accurate, since an author might write only, say, poems or essays that are never collected into a book, let's say an author is someone who writes a text. But we immediately see that this is not quite right either. A text is any thing written at all, including shopping lists, notes passed in class, emails to the phone company about my bill. Having written such things, as we all have, does not make one an author. As Foucault suggests, even when we aim at collecting 'everything' by a great author such as Nietzsche, we do not include these texts. Only certain kinds of texts count as the 'work' of an author.

Our definition has another weakness. Someone may literally write a text, even one of the 'right sort', and not be its author. This is obviously the case if a text is dictated to a secretary, but it is also true, if more complexly so, of other cases: when, for example, a film star writes an autobiography 'with the assistance of' or 'as told to' someone; or when a politician 'writes' a column or gives a speech that has been produced by a team of aides; or when a scientist is 'first author' on a paper coming from his lab but in fact has not himself written a single word of it. Such cases make it clear that being an author is not, as our simple definition assumed, just a matter of being the literal 'cause' (producer) of a certain kind of text. It is instead a matter of being judged *responsible* for the text. As Foucault notes, different cultures have had different standards for assigning such responsibility. In the ancient world, for example, all medical texts accepted as having a certain level of authority were designated as the works of a canonical author such as Hippocrates. On the other hand, there have been periods in which literary texts (such as poems and stories) were circulated anonymously and not regarded as texts to which we should assign an author (compare jokes in our culture).

From both these kinds of considerations—those about the sorts of texts that can have an author and those about the sort of responsibility for a text that makes someone an author of it—Foucault concludes that we should, strictly, not speak of the 'author' but of the 'author function'. To be an author is not merely to have a certain factual relation to a text (for example, to have causally produced it); it is, rather, to fulfil a certain socially and culturally defined role in relation to the text. Authorship is a social construction, not a natural kind, and it will vary over cultures and over time.

Foucault further maintains that the author function, as it operates in a given text, does not correspond to a single self (person) who is the author of that text. There is, for any 'authored' text, a plurality of selves fulfilling the author function. So, in a first-person novel, the 'I' who narrates is different from the person who actually wrote the words the 'I' presents, but both have a fair claim to being the 'author'. The classic example is Proust's *À la recherche du temps perdu*, with its complex interplay between 'Marcel', the narrative voice, and Proust 'himself'. Foucault finds the same plurality in a mathematical treatise, where we must distinguish the 'I' of the preface, who thanks her husband for his support, and the theorem-proving 'I' of the main text who writes 'I suppose' or 'I conclude'. Of course, there is a single author in the obvious sense that one person wrote the words of the text. But, as an author, this person assumes a variety of roles, corresponding to a diversity of selves: 'the author function operates so as to effect the dispersion of these...simultaneous selves' ('What Is an Author?', EW I, 216).

We see already that the role of an author might well attract someone like Foucault who does not want to be fixed in a single identity. But there are deeper ways in which writing can move me away from myself. To see this, let us return to our initial common-sense model of the author as the person who writes a text. We have so far seen complications with the identity of the author. But there are also difficulties for our common-sense idea that authors (however understood) produce (cause) the texts they write. Foucault neatly formulated the issue in *The Order of Things*. Nietzsche, he said, showed us the importance of always asking of a text 'Who is speaking?' (who—from what historical position, with what particular interests—is claiming the authority to be listened to?). But, Foucault continues, Mallarmé responded to this question, at least as it concerns literature: it is 'the word itself'

(OT, 305). Are there, as Mallarmé suggests, senses in which a text is due to the word, to language itself, rather than to its author?

Of course there are. Every language embodies a rich conceptual structure that dictates at every turn how I speak and even what I say. Shakespearean English is an excellent vehicle for discussing the sport of falconry but not of football. The fact that Shakespeare's plays contain fluent and complex treatments of falconry is due as much to the resources of Elizabethan English as to Shakespeare's interest in the topic. If Shakespeare came back to life to attend a final in the World Cup, he would, great writer that he is, be severely handicapped in giving an accurate account of the game. Our accounts of a football match would be far superior to Shakespeare's, not because of our greater literary ability but because of the language we have available to us.

But, you may say, this is just an accident, due to the fact that football did not exist in Shakespeare's day, and one that can easily be remedied by adding an Elizabethan sub-vocabulary suitable for describing football matches. True, but, first, any language that we can actually use has to be at some specific point in its historical development and will have limitations accordingly. Second, it may be that there are fundamental limitations in the structure of any particular language that make it simply incapable of certain sorts of expression. Indeed, it seems likely that this is so—that, for example, there are things in Goethe's or Rilke's German that simply cannot be adequately put into English. Heidegger maintained—though it is hard to see how he could know—that only ancient Greek and German were adequate for the discussion of philosophy.

Accordingly, when authors write, much of what they say is a product not of their distinctive insight or ability but the result of the language they are employing. For much of the text it is just language that is speaking. Authors can react to this fact in different ways. One standard (romantic) idea sees the author as straining against the structures of language to express unique individual insights. Here the assumption is that an author has access to a personal, prelinguistic vision, the expression of which must work against language's tendency to merely conventional expression. A contrary 'classical' idea sees the author as accepting and deploying the standard structures to craft yet another work embodying a traditional vision. Both the classical and the romantic views present writing as a matter of individuals *expressing* themselves; they differ only over whether what is expressed should be the author's own personal vision or the author's appropriation of a tradition. Foucault, however, is especially interested in another mode in which authors can relate to language, one in which the point is not to use language for self-expression but to lose the self in language.

This sort of authorship corresponds to a certain sense of literary modernism, associated with the 'death of the author'—although, as our discussion has shown, this is really just the death of the conception of the author as self-expressive. Replacing it is the idea of an author as a vehicle for letting language reveal itself. This idea, however, is less prominent in 'What Is an Author?' than in some of Foucault's subsequent discussions. In *The Order of Things,* for example, he says: 'The whole curiosity of our thought now resides in the question: What is language, how can we find a way around it in order to make it appear in itself, in all its plentitude?' (OT, 306).

The notion is particularly prominent in Foucault's inaugural address for his chair at the Collège de France (titled *L'ordre du discours,* but oddly translated into English as 'The Discourse on Language'). Here we see the strongly personal resonance of this theme for Foucault, as he is required to give a public address: 'I would', he begins, 'really like to have slipped imperceptibly into this lecture...I would have preferred to be enveloped in words...At the moment of speaking, I would like to have perceived a nameless voice, long preceding me, leaving me merely

13

to enmesh myself in it...' (DL, 215). Foucault associates himself with the modernist voice of Beckett's Molloy: 'I must go on; I can't go on; I must go on; I must say words as long as there are words, I must say them until they find me, until they say me...' (Samuel Beckett, *The Unnameable*, quoted in DL, 215). Later in the lecture, he argues that the notion of the author as 'the unifying principle in a group of writings or statement, lying at the origins of their significance, as the seat of their coherence' (DL, 221) is less a source of creative expression than a principle of limitation, forcing us to read a text as conforming with a comprehensive authorial project. At the very end, he elegantly turns these theoretical flights back to the occasion at hand, saying that the voice he was wishing for, 'preceding me, supporting me, inviting me to speak and lodging within my own speech', was in fact that of Jean Hyppolite, his revered former teacher and immediate predecessor in the Chair of Philosophy at the Collège de France (DL, 237). But it remains clear that, for Foucault, language can and must take us beyond the mode of subjective or even inter-subjective expression.

But in what sense might language offer us a truth beyond our subjective selves? There is, of course, the fact that language provides the framework of our daily existence, through structures that are, so to speak, too close for us to notice. Anglophone ordinary-language philosophy, following Wittgenstein in the 1950s and 1960s, offered one way of uncovering this linguistic 'unconscious'. The 'archaeology of knowledge' Foucault developed in the 1960s offered another, much more historical way. But the thread of his thought that we are currently following is not concerned with language as a substructure of everyday life. Here his fascination is rather with writing that puts extreme pressure on language, that presses it to its limits with paradox, and that, as a result, produces experiences of violation and transgression.

A premier example of such writing is that of Georges Bataille (Figure 3), about whom Foucault wrote his passionately obscure

3. Georges Bataille.

essay 'A Preface to Transgression'. Sexuality, the primary theme of Bataille's violently pornographic fiction, is a primary locus of transgression because it is implicated in all of our limit-experiences (Foucault's term for experiences of transgression, those that take us to or beyond the limits of intelligibility and propriety). Pushing consciousness to its limits leads to the unconscious, which after Freud we all know is a maelstrom of sexual desires. The limit of the laws of human societies is the universal taboo of incest. And the limits of language, specifying, in Foucault's words, 'just how far speech may advance upon the sands of silence' ('A Preface to Transgression', EW II, 70), are, of course, always marked by the 'forbidden words' of sexuality.

Pornographic writing is typically a very conservative medium, of course, a series of clichés, clogged with erotic associations that

15

stimulate desire, but not offering new modes of experience or thought. Bataille's pornography, however, is less likely to arouse than to shock, repel, and dazzle through the extremity of its images, all the more disturbing because they are expressed in classically limpid prose. It is further intensified by the paradox implicit in the post-Nietzschean world Bataille inhabits. In this world, God is dead, which means that there are no objectively defined limits of thought or action against which we can hurl ourselves. 'Profanation in a world that no longer recognizes any positive meaning in the sacred—is this not more or less what we may call transgression?' Our limits are ones that we know are set by ourselves, so passing beyond (transgressing) them can only mean rebelling against ourselves, via 'a profanation that is empty and turned inward upon itself, whose instruments are brought to bear on nothing but each other' (EW II, 70). But the very absurdity of this effort heightens the limit-experience through its defiance of the very laws of logic.

The point of this exercise in extremism is to release forces within language that will hurl us to the limits of our ordinary concepts and experiences and give us a (perhaps transforming) glimpse of radically new modes of thought. In all this, Bataille the author can claim no access to special infra- or ultra-rational insight from another world (he was, after all, in real life the most mundane of men: a head librarian at the Bibliothèque Nationale). But his writing is designed to unleash from language new transgressive truths that will take him and his readers beyond the realm of their knowledge and capacity of expression.

But Bataille's pornographic violence is by no means the only way to make a space for language itself to speak. Whereas his prose flows from an excess of subjectivity, from erotic fantasy incited to extraordinary limits, the writing of Maurice Blanchot shimmers with a strangeness that seems due to the complete withdrawal of all subjectivity. As Foucault reads him, Blanchot is a master of the 'thought of the outside', a thought (or even an experience) that, just as in Bataille, embodies 'the breakdown of philosophical subjectivity and its dispersion in a language that dispossesses it while multiplying it within the space created by its absence' ('A Preface to Transgression', EW II, 79). Foucault traces this experience from Sade and Hölderlin through Nietzsche and Mallarmé to Artaud, Bataille, and Klossowski, to a culmination in Blanchot, who, he says, 'is perhaps more than just another witness to this thought'. For, while his predecessors have expressed the thought of the outside by, in their various ways, separating language from its roots in divine and human consciousness, Blanchot is so completely absent from his texts that 'for us he is that thought itself—its real, absolutely distant, shimmering, invisible presence, its necessary destiny, its inevitable law, its calm, infinite, measured strength' ('The Thought of the Outside', EW II, 151). We might say that to Bataille's ecstatic of violation there corresponds Blanchot's ascetic of withdrawal. In the paradoxes of limit-experience, the two are equivalent. For both—though Foucault may think more purely and decisively in Blanchot—the central and controlling subject is replaced by language itself. Not language as the instrument or expression of consciousness, but language 'in its attentive and forgetful being, with its power of dissimulation that effaces every determinate meaning and even the existence of the speaker' (EW II, 168).

Transgression, paradox, and the dispersion of subjectivity all converge on the ultimate limit-experience of madness itself, of those who have, as we say, 'gone off the deep end'. We will discuss Foucault's rich and provocative treatment of madness later, but it will be no surprise that he took special interest in the works of 'mad' authors such as Nietzsche, Artaud, and Raymond Roussel (all of whom were at one point or another clinically diagnosed as insane). Foucault, however, emphasizes that even in these cases the writer's achievement is never literally that of a madman. 'Madness', he reminds us, 'is precisely the absence of the work of art' (MC, 287). Full-blown insanity makes significant writing impossible, and we do not, for example, consider Nietzsche's last mad postcards from Turin (signed 'Christ' and 'Dionysus') as parts of his oeuvre. The privilege and special interest of 'mad' writers is due to their liminal position at the border of the sane world. Their writing operates in the twilight zone between coherence and incoherence, their mental 'disturbances' effecting the transgression and withdrawal that Bataille and Blanchot achieve by more deliberate means. We saw in Chapter 1 how Roussel used arbitrary restrictions to open the way for writing that was not driven by any intentions of expressing the author's ideas and that cleared a field for an essentially unguided unfolding of a linguistic structure. Other authors, influenced by Roussel, have used similar devices, particularly members of the Oulipo group (*Ouvroir de littérature potentielle*) such as Raymond Queneau, Georges Perec, Italo Calvino, and Harry Mathews. The most famous example is Perec's *La disparition*, a novel written in French without a single use of the letter 'e'.

Foucault's fascination with avant-garde literature is an aspect of his tendency to seek, in extreme (limit-) experiences, a truth and fulfilment beyond that of ordinary existence. As he said in an interview (just two years before his death):

> those middle-range pleasures that make up everyday life...are nothing for me...A pleasure must be something incredibly intense...Some drugs are really important for me because they are the mediations to those incredibly intense joys that I'm looking for.
>
> ('Michel Foucault: An Interview by Stephen Riggins', EW I, 129)

But while this lure of intensity remained important for Foucault as a private individual, he seems, after the 1960s (when he wrote almost all of his literary essays), to have gradually become less convinced that limit-experiences and the literature that evokes them were the keys to transforming society. Instead, he moved to a much more political conception of what was needed to effect human liberation. In Chapter 3, we will follow this thread of Foucault's thought.

Chapter 3
Politics

Michel Foucault was quite proud of the fact that he was difficult to classify politically:

> I think I have in fact been situated in most of the squares of the political checkerboard, one after another and sometimes simultaneously: as an anarchist, leftist, ostentatious or disguised Marxist, technocrat in the service of Gaullism, new liberal, and so forth...None of these descriptions is important by itself; taken together, on the other hand, they mean something. And I must admit that I rather like what they mean.

('Polemics, Politics, and Problematizations', EW III, 115)

Although Foucault was away in Tunisia during the student revolts of May 1968, Maurice Blanchot reports having seen and spoken to him at a demonstration at this time. If so, this was the only encounter between Foucault and the man he said he once 'dreamt of being'. Whether or not the story is true—Foucault may have returned for a few days that summer—it works nicely as a symbol of the tension between the aesthetic and the political in Foucault's life and thought. Perhaps he met his literary hero only at the very point at which he began to move away from high art as our saving liberation to an acceptance of the mundane political sphere as the inevitable battleground for human freedom. At any rate,

Foucault's attitude changed at the end of the 1960s and, by 1977, he was speaking of modernist literary theory in the past tense, noting that the wave of interest in the 1960s (with critics such as Barthes, writers such as Sollers, and journals such as *Tel Quel*) amounted to its swan song. What Foucault failed to mention was that he was an important voice in that chorus.

There may be no need to see Foucault's writings as taking a radically new direction in the 1970s. His own suggestion—'I ask myself what else it was I was talking about in *Madness and Civilization* and *The Birth of the Clinic*, but power'—has some plausibility, though he goes on to say that he did not have the conceptual tools to thematize power in his book on madness ('Truth and Power', EW III, 117). But there is no doubt that after 1968 his work had a directly political cast that corresponded, in his life outside writing, to a much increased activism.

Particularly since World War II—if not since the Dreyfus Affair or the French Revolution—there has been a strong political tone to French intellectual life. Abstruse philosophical or sociological treatises are denounced or praised because of their perceived *prises de position* on political issues of the day. This attitude is especially apparent in Jean-Paul Sartre's insistence that writing must be committed *(engagée)*. *La littérature engagée* is, for Sartre, writing that recognizes its inevitable relation to its historical situation and strives to make its readers aware of and act on the potential for human liberation implicit in that situation. Such writing is not, Sartre maintains, mere propaganda because it is not the servant of any specific ideology but expresses the 'eternal values implicit in social and political debates' *(Situations II, 15)*.

Foucault, like all the intellectuals of his generation, grew up under the shadow of Sartre, and his politics in particular need to be understood vis-à-vis Sartre, whose defining political experience was the war and the German occupation of France. This experience led Sartre to see political decisions in the absolute

terms of loyalty and betrayal, corresponding to the stark choice either to support the Resistance or to collaborate. As he put it: 'whatever the circumstances, and wherever the site, a man is always free to choose to be a traitor or not'. (Much later, when an interviewer showed him this passage, he said that 'when I read this, I said to myself: it's incredible, I actually believed that!' and attributed his attitude to the 'drama of the war and the experience of heroism'—*Between Existentialism and Marxism*, 33–4.)
Another lesson of the war—and not just in Sartre's mind—was the morally and politically privileged position of the French Communist Party. As the vanguard of the Resistance, the Communists had earned the gratitude and respect of even those French who did not sympathize with their political and social goals. For leftist intellectuals like Sartre (Figure 4), the Communists had an unquestionable credibility in post-war France. This did not entail membership in the Party, and Sartre himself never joined. But for a long time the Communists' agenda dominated his political thought and activity, and there was a period in the 1950s when, whatever his private reservations, his

4. Foucault and Sartre at a demonstration in Paris, 27 November 1972.

public stance was one of total support for the Party, even at the price of breaking with his friends Albert Camus and Maurice Merleau-Ponty. It is no surprise that he came to see Marxism as 'the one philosophy of our time which we cannot go beyond' (*Critique of Dialectical Reason*, xxxiv).

Foucault, born twenty-one years after Sartre, did not experience the war as a politically awakened adult but as a confused adolescent. Coming to maturity in the political instability and ambiguity of post-war France, he was sceptical of Sartre's ethical and political absolutes and questioned the pretensions of what he came to call, with Sartre clearly in mind, the 'universal intellectual', a free spirit, 'the spokesman of the universal', 'speaking in the capacity of master of truth and justice' ('Truth and Power', EW III, 126). This was no doubt once a worthy calling, but today, according to Foucault, universal systems of morality no longer provide effective responses to social and political problems. We need detailed responses formulated by those concretely involved in the problems. This, Foucault maintains, is the domain of the 'specific intellectual', for example the teacher, engineer, doctor, or consultant who 'has at his disposal, whether in the service of the State or against it, powers which can benefit or irrevocably destroy life' (EW III, 129)—not Sartre but Oppenheimer.

It is sometimes suggested that Foucault saw himself as a specific intellectual, but (apart from his early work in psychiatric hospitals) he did not generally have that sort of particular responsibility in the social system. Call him rather—though he himself does not use the term—a 'critical intellectual', someone who does not speak with the authority of universal principles or of specific social or political responsibilities but simply on the basis of his historical erudition and analytical skills. Neither 'the rhapsodist of the eternal' nor 'the strategist of life and death' (EW III, 129), the critical intellectual provides the intellectual tools—awarenesses of strategic and tactical possibilities—those in the political trenches need to fight their battles.

Foucault's most obvious political separation from Sartre appears in his attitude toward Marxism and the Communist Party that was its primary representative. Early on, Foucault did feel the tug of the Marxist viewpoint. 'I belong', he told an interviewer, 'to that generation who as students had before their eyes, and were limited by, a horizon consisting of Marxism, phenomenology, and existentialism' (RR, interview, 174). (The influence of existential phenomenology—especially of the early Heidegger—on Foucault is most apparent in his long introduction to the French translation of Ludwig Binswanger's essay *Traum und Existenz.*) Particularly because of the influence at the École Normale of Louis Althusser, who was the leading theoretician of the French Communist Party, Foucault's early intellectual attachment to Marxism was strong. In his first book, *Maladie mentale et personnalité,* he characterized non-Marxist approaches, including the existential, as providing only 'mythical explanations', and maintained that mental illnesses arise ultimately from 'contradictions' determined by 'present economic conditions in the form of conflict, exploitation, imperialist wars, and class struggle' (86). In one sense, Foucault went even further than Sartre, and was for a time a member of the French Communist Party. But he was very soon disillusioned with both the theory and the practice of Marxism. He quit the Party after only 'a few months or a little more' ('Michel Foucault répond à Sartre', DE I, 666)—in fact, it was closer to a year—and, in a 1962 second edition of his book on mental illness (retitled *Maladie mentale et psychologie),* covered his tracks. He eliminated almost all Marxist elements, including his entire concluding chapter, which had argued that Pavlov's theory of the reflex was the key to understanding mental illness, and added an entirely new historical dimension based on his just-published doctoral thesis, *The History of Madness.*

Foucault's subsequent attitude toward Marxism was complexly ambivalent. *The Order of Things,* for example, made the shocking claim that Marx's economic thought was not at root original or revolutionary, that the controversies it occasioned 'are no more than storms in a children's wading pool' (OT, 262). But when pressed on this point in a later interview, he explained that he was speaking only of Marx's significance for the specific domain of economics, not of his unquestionably major role in social theory ('Sur les façons d'écrire l'histoire', interview with Raymond Bellour, DE I, 587). It is hard to avoid the conclusion that, throughout his writings, Foucault took Marxism quite seriously but was quite happy to tweak the pretentious sensibilities of contemporary French Marxists, for whose sake he would introduce teasing remarks into his writings and interviews. So, for example, he says, to the reproach that he doesn't cite the text of Marx in places where this would be appropriate, that of course he does refer quite obviously to Marx on many occasions, but doesn't bother to give explicit footnotes to guide those who don't know their Marx well enough to pick up the reference (P/K, 'Prison Talk', 52). On the other hand, Foucault is quite explicit in acknowledging in *Discipline and Punish* the importance of the Marxist work of Rusche and Kirchheimer for his history of the prison.

Foucault's most direct statement of his attitude toward Marxism occurs in an interview with Paul Rabinow about a month before his death: 'I am neither an adversary nor a partisan of Marxism; I question it about what it has to say about experiences that ask questions of it' ('Polemics, Politics, and Problematizations', EW I, 115). Here Foucault is treating Marxism as an example of what, in this interview, he calls 'politics', by which he seems to mean a general, theoretically informed framework for discussing current political issues. His point is that such frameworks should never be simply assumed as an adequate basis for political decisions, but should be regarded merely as resources that may (or may not) suggest viable approaches to problems we face. Here he cites the paradigm example of the 1968 student revolt, which, he insists, involved asking a set of questions—'about women, about relations between the sexes, about medicine, about the environment, about minorities, about delinquency'—that were not traditionally treated by established political viewpoints such as Marxism. At the same time, he notes, the student activists seemed to assume that Marxism was the proper vehicle for discussing these questions: 'there was a desire to rewrite all these problems in the vocabulary of a theory that was derived more or less directly from Marxism'. But, he concludes, Marxism was inadequate to the task: there was 'a more and more manifest powerlessness on the part of Marxism to confront these problems'. On the positive side, he concludes, we had learned that serious political questions could be raised independently of accepted political doctrines ('politics') so that, as a result, 'now there was a plurality of questions posed to politics rather than the reinscription of the act of questioning in the framework of a political doctrine' (EW I, 115).

Foucault generalizes his point in a political distinction between *polemics* and *problematizations*. Polemics comes to political issues with a general doctrinal framework it accepts as the only adequate basis for discussion. Anyone who does not accept the framework is treated as an enemy who must be refuted, not as a partner in the search for a solution. Like parallel enterprises in religion (the eradication of heresy) and the judiciary (criminal prosecution), polemics 'defines alliances, recruits partisans, unites interests or opinions, represents a party; it establishes the other as an enemy, an upholder of opposed interests against which one must fight until the moment this enemy is defeated' (EW I, 112). (It is hard not to recall Sartre's pledge of allegiance to the Communist cause: 'an anticommunist is a rat...I swore to the bourgeoisie a hatred which would only die with me', 'Merleau-Ponty', in *Situations*, 198.) Foucault rejects polemics as 'sterilizing': 'Has anyone ever seen a new idea come out of a polemic?' Moreover, 'it is really dangerous to make anyone believe that he can gain access to truth by such paths and thus to validate, even if merely in a symbolic form, the real political practices that could be warranted by it'. Ordinarily, Foucault says, the worst consequences of the polemical attitude 'remain suspended', presumably because there is no decisive victor among the warring viewpoints. But, he says, we know what happens when one side is able to triumph: 'one has

25

only to look at what happened during the debates in the USSR over linguistics or genetics not long ago' (EW I, 113).

Problematization does not ignore the doctrinal frameworks of polemical disputes—which are after all a primary source for our thinking about political questions. But it begins with questions that arise not necessarily from the frameworks themselves but from our 'lived experiences' in society. We can and should put these questions not only to the doctrinal frameworks (to 'politics'), but also to a variety of frameworks and with no assumption that all or any of them will offer adequate answers. Political discussions should be driven by the concrete problems that raise our questions, not by the established theories that claim to be able to answer them.

Foucault also makes his point in Richard Rorty's pragmatic language of the 'we' (group consensus)—and at the same time responds to an important challenge to his approach to politics. Rorty, Foucault notes, has pointed out that Foucault's political analyses 'do not appeal to any 'we'—to any of those *'wes'* whose consensus, whose values, whose traditions constitute the framework for a thought' (EW I, 114). Rorty's worry was that, by not beginning from any consensus, Foucault (Figure 5) was confusing the private and public domains of discourse and seeking a public endorsement of values (for example, the pursuit of intense limit-experiences) that are appropriate only as part of an individual's self-creation, not as the norms of a liberal society. Foucault's response is, in effect, that the 'we' is essential, but as an outcome not a presupposition of political discussion: 'it seems to me that the 'we' must not be previous to the question, it can only be the result—and the necessarily temporary result—of the question as it is posed in the new terms in which one formulates it' (EW I, 114–15).

This is an effective response but one that implicitly concedes a key point of Rorty's challenge. The questions that precede and

5. Foucault circa 1969.

generate political consensus must, of course, themselves be ones
that can be formulated in the mundane vocabularies of everyday
discourse; otherwise they would not even be candidates for
subsequently agreed-upon answers. But this means that
'inexpressible' limit-experiences, whatever their role in private
lives, can have no place in the public forum of political discussion.
Foucault can deny Rorty's assumption that political discussion
must begin from substantial agreement (say on the liberal political
creed), but he must also admit that Rorty is right about the
political irrelevance of the irreducibly private values on which
Foucault placed so much emphasis in his early aesthetic writings.

If political debate is not grounded in theoretical frameworks, it is
fair to ask to what authority it does appeal. Often, of course, we
can get along without raising questions about the ultimate

27

justification of values; the factual questions of how to achieve certain goals are foregrounded against the backdrop of implicit shared commitments. In such cases, we might say, the issues are ones of pragmatic reform rather than fundamental revolution. Foucault, however, rejected the separability of questions of reform (transformation), working within an established system, and the revolutionary critique of the system. Discussing with Didier Eribon the election of François Mitterrand's socialist government in 1981, Foucault resisted Eribon's suggestion that his sympathy with the opening moves of the new regime meant that he thought it would be 'possible to work with this government' ('So Is It Important to Think?', EW III, 455). He rejected 'the dilemma of being either for or against' and went on to argue that even reformist projects (within a system) require 'criticism (and radical criticism)', since any reform worthy of the name requires questioning modes of thought that say it is impossible. Accordingly, we cannot choose between 'an inaccessible radicality' and 'the necessary concessions to reality'. Rather, 'the work of deep transformation [reform] can be done in the open and always turbulent atmosphere of a continuous [revolutionary] criticism' (EW III, 457).

But this position makes all the more insistent the question of what grounds fundamental criticisms of existing regimes, since for Foucault such criticism should be a constant of political life, not just of special moments of revolutionary upheaval. We can get a sense of Foucault's response to this question by examining his controversial discussion of the Iranian revolution, with which he expressed an early sympathy that disconcerted many. But Foucault's sympathy was with the basic act of revolt: 'the impulse by which a single individual, a group, a minority, or an entire people says, "I will no longer obey," and throws the risk of their life in the face of an authority they consider unjust' ('Useless to Revolt?', EW III, 449). Such an act, he says, is 'irreducible' and even an 'escape' from 'history, and its long chains of reasons'. The decision 'to prefer the risk of death to the certainty of having to obey' is the 'last anchor point' for any assertions of rights, 'one more solid and closer to experience than "natural rights"' (EW III, 449).

But, the philosopher in us will ask, what is the status of this will to revolt? No doubt there is a kind of authenticity in the acceptance of death as the possible price of freedom, but, as Foucault puts it, 'Is one right to revolt, or not?' At least in this discussion, he avoids answering: 'Let us leave the question open. People do revolt; that is a fact...A question of ethics? Perhaps. A question of reality, without a doubt.' All he is willing to say is that it is only through such revolt that 'subjectivity (not that of great men, but that of anyone) is brought into history' (EW III, 452), making human lives not just a matter of biological evolution but genuinely historical, and that his commitment as an intellectual is 'to be respectful when a singularity revolts, intransigent as soon as power violates the universal' (EW III, 453).

Not a very satisfactory response, we might say, especially when we recall that the revolution in question is one that led directly to a tyranny of stonings and severed hands. Foucault admits that the Iranian revolution contained, from the beginning, seeds of its own atrocities: 'the formidable hope of making Islam into a great civilization once again, and forms of virulent xenophobia'. He insists, however, that 'the spirituality which had meaning for those who went to their deaths has no common measure with the bloody government of an integrist clergy' (EW III, 451). But wasn't the spirit of revolt equally in those who died and those who lived to tyrannize? And isn't there every reason to think that a reversal of fates would have turned the martyrs into clerical tyrants? How can we be 'respectful' of revolts that we have every reason to think will lead to a new tyranny? Foucault says there is no inconsistency 'when today one is against severed hands, having yesterday been against the tortures of the Savak' (EW III, 452). But why respect a movement opposing the Savak when you have good reason to believe that it will lead to equal outrages?

In other places, Foucault employs the category of the 'intolerable' to characterize practices or situations that are the legitimate objects of resistance or revolt. This has the advantage of allowing us to differentiate some instances of revolt as morally appropriate (because they oppose what is intolerable) and others as not. Foucault's 'respect' for the Iranian revolution may reflect his reluctance to judge a case of obviously sincere commitment that he could not know from the inside. Presumably, he would act differently regarding movements within his own culture, where he would be in a position to judge whether or not what they opposed was intolerable. But there is no doubt that he would see such a judgement as itself an irreducible given, not the outcome of the application of the theoretical categories of a political or other ethical framework. In the end, there can be no authority other than the judgement of those who directly experience a situation.

Chapter 4
Archaeology

Foucault is often treated as a philosopher, social theorist, or cultural critic, but in fact almost all of his books were histories, from *The History of Madness* to the *History of Sexuality;* and when the Collège de France asked for a title for his chair, his choice was 'Professor of the History of Systems of Thought'. Nonetheless, he saw his historical work as quite different from standard work in history of ideas and characterized it in distinctive terms, first as the 'archaeology' of thought and later as 'genealogy'.

Foucault's idea of an archaeology of thought is closely linked to the modernist literary idea that language is a source of thought in its own right, not merely an instrument for expressing the ideas of those who use it. Here, however, the project is not to open up, through transgression or withdrawal, a field for language itself to 'speak'. Rather, Foucault begins with the fact that, at any given period in a given domain, there are substantial constraints on how people are able to think. Of course, there are always the formal constraints of grammar and logic, which exclude certain formulations as gibberish (meaningless) or illogical (self-contradictory). But what the archaeologist of thought is interested in is a further set of constraints that, for example, make it 'unthinkable' for centuries that heavenly bodies could move other than in circles or be made of earthly material. Such constraints seem foolish to us: why couldn't they see that such things are at least possible? But Foucault's idea is that every mode of thinking involves implicit rules (maybe not even formulable by those following them) that materially restrict the range of thought. If we can uncover these rules, we will be able to see how an apparently arbitrary constraint actually makes total sense in the framework defined by those rules. Moreover, he suggests that our own thinking too is governed by such rules, so that from the vantage point of the future it will look quite as arbitrary as the past does to us.

Foucault's idea is that this level of analysis, of what is outside the control of the individuals who actually do the thinking in a given period, is the key to understanding the constraints within which people think. So the 'history of ideas'—where this means what is consciously going on in the minds of scientists, philosophers, et al.—is less important than the underlying structures that form the context for their thinking. We will not be so much interested in, say, Hume or Darwin as in what made Hume or Darwin possible. This is the root of Foucault's famous 'marginalization of the subject'. It is not that he denies the reality or even the supreme ethical importance of the individual consciousness. But he thinks that individuals operate in a conceptual environment that determines and limits them in ways of which they cannot be aware.

There are, besides archaeology, two other plausible metaphors for Foucault's new intellectual enterprise: geology and psychoanalysis. Sartre suggested the geological analogy, and Foucault himself employs it when he speaks of the 'sedimentary strata' (AK, 3) uncovered by the kind of historical approach he proposes. But this metaphor misleadingly suggests that we can, like the geologist, actually reach and 'see for ourselves' the underlying structures of thought, whereas all we actually have access to are the surface effects (specific uses of language) from which we must somehow infer what lies beneath. The psychoanalytic metaphor, which Foucault himself emphasizes, rightly presents the underlying structures as part of an unconscious and as discovered only through analysis of linguistic events of which we are aware. But, unlike psychoanalysis, Foucault's history is not hermeneutic; that is, it does not try to *interpret* what we hear and read in order to recover its deeper meaning. It deals with texts but treats them not as documents but, in the manner of an archaeologist, as monuments (AK, 7). Archaeologists of knowledge, in other words, do not ask what Descartes' *Meditations* mean (that is, what ideas Descartes was trying to express in them). Rather, they use what Descartes—and many other writers, famous or not, of the same period—wrote as clues to the general structure of the system in which they thought and wrote. The interest, to invoke the archaeological analogy once more, is not in the particular object (text) studied but in the overall configuration of the site from which it was excavated.

Just as the modernist avant-garde aimed at writing without the author, so Foucault's archaeology aims at history without the individual subject. Contrary to what is often suggested, this does not mean the total exclusion of the subject from history; Foucault is, after all, talking about *our* history. But archaeology emphasizes that the stage on which we enact our history—as well as much of the script—is established independently of our thoughts and actions. This separates it from conventional history, which tells of individual subjects moving through time. Standard history of ideas, in particular, tells how philosophers, scientists, and other thinkers developed and transmitted to their successors key concepts and theories. Foucault does not exclude such 'subject-centred' accounts, but he points out that they are prone to characteristic distortions. They treat history as a story, a narrative, which, since it is told from the standpoint of one or more person's experiences, assumes the continuity and goal-directedness of consciousness. History thus becomes a novel, with a plot unified by the concerns of human beings and leading to a humanly meaningful conclusion. Such narration has a superficial validity, but it ignores the extent to which the apparent continuity and purposiveness of history may be due to the false assumption that human history is primarily driven by the experiences and projects of the consciousnesses that live it. Archaeology introduces factors outside consciousness that may belie the continuity and direction that we read into our lives.

To illustrate Foucault's point, consider the much abused 'Whiggish' interpretations of history, which tell a tale of gradual progress toward our glorious present. (The term 'Whiggish' refers to the ideology of the Whig Party, which permeates Lord Macaulay's famous *History of England*.) While 20th-century historians denigrate the naiveté of assuming that the past should be read as a continual progress toward ourselves as its manifest purpose, their alternative has typically been to tell the story of a past time in terms of its own conceptions and concerns—a narrative of 'how-it-then-seemed-to-them'. But why, for example, should the Elizabethans' perspective on their history be privileged over Lord Macaulay's, and why should either be privileged over, say, that of the biological, meteorological, or geographic factors that may well have had far more influence on their history than anything the Elizabethans thought? This, indeed, was the approach that proved so fruitful for the French *Annales* school of historiography (named after its journal), which Foucault cites very positively at the opening of *The Archaeology of Knowledge*, where he reflects on his own effort to extend the *Annales* methodology to the history of thought.

We may object that such an extension is incoherent, since, obviously, what the Elizabethans thought was decisive for the history of their thought. Foucault, however, is precisely questioning the alleged truism. The archaeologist suggests that much of 'what the Elizabethans thought'—in the normal sense of 'what ideas they were consciously aware of'—may have been the rather distant outcome of factors quite outside their consciousness. On the other hand, Foucault is not pursuing the project of explaining ideas by external social or economic forces, in the manner of Marxism or other forms of historical materialism. His project is rather to offer an *internal* account of human thinking, without assuming a privileged status for the conscious content of that thought—thought without a privileged role for the thinker, parallel to writing without a privileged role for the writer. And, as in the case of modernist literature, the key to this project is language, conceived as a structure independent of those who use it. This suggests yet another analogy helpful for understanding Foucault's project—it is like Chomsky's linguistics, which tries to uncover the 'deep structure' of our language. Foucault, however, is not concerned with formal (syntactic or semantic) structures but those that constrain the material content of what is said and thought.

This notion of 'constraining' thought suggests one final disciplinary analogy for the archaeology of thought: the effort, characteristic of so much philosophy since Kant, to determine the 'conditions of possibility' of our concepts and experience. Kant called these conditions 'transcendental' because they are neither empirical (that is, due to the contingent history of human life) nor transcendent (that is, due to necessary constraints imposed on us from outside). Rather, they are conditions necessary, given our situation as finite knowers, for our being able to have any experience at all of a world. On Kant's view, the transcendental conditions on the possibility of experience require, for example, that we experience objects as existing in space and time and as substances subject to causal laws. Since such conditions are prior to experience, Kant called them 'a priori' (as opposed to the 'a posteriori' truths that are derived from our experience).

Foucault sometimes characterized his archaeological project in Kantian language, saying that it sought the 'conditions of possibility' for thought in a given period (OT, xxii). For Kant, however, such conditions were universally applicable, necessary constraints on all possible experiences, whereas for Foucault they are contingent on the particular historical situation and vary over times and domains of knowledge. The concept of invariant species was a necessary condition for the knowledge of life in the 18th century but not the 20th. Consequently, Foucault says that archaeology leads to only relativized 'historical *a prioris*', not the atemporal, absolute a priori truths that Kant claimed to have discovered. This difference is deep, since Kant's claims of universal necessity required his transcendental project to invoke methods beyond those of empirical studies such as natural science and history; they required a distinctively philosophical a priori method of transcendental argument. Foucault may employ Kant's terminology, but his project seeks no truths beyond those available to the empirical methods of historiography.

Foucault's archaeology leads to some striking challenges to received ideas in the history of science. It is, for example, commonly held that Lamarck anticipated Darwin's evolutionary ideas, whereas Cuvier was solidly opposed to the thought of species emerging through gradual changes over a long period. In *The Order of Things*, Foucault agrees that Lamarck speaks of species changing over time (through the inheritance of acquired characteristics), whereas Cuvier's theory posits species that are fixed once and for all. But he maintains that these conflicting opinions cover up a more fundamental division. Lamarck works within a general archaeological framework (an 'episteme' in Foucault's terminology) associated with the 'Classical Age' (roughly, Europe—and especially France—from 1650 to 1800). According to Foucault's analysis, the Classical episteme allows no essential role for time in its view of nature. All the possible kinds of living things are predetermined in total independence of historical developments and can be expressed entirely in atemporal tables of genera and species. The actualization of genera and species in time need not realize all the possibilities simultaneously, but the order of their appearance would have to be strictly in accord with the atemporal relations specified by the tables of genera and species. Lamarck postulated such a process of successive realization, but had (and could have) no idea of there being *historical causes* that produced the differences in species that came to exist at different times.

Cuvier, admittedly, claimed that in fact all species had existed from the beginning and so were not produced by historical causes. But, unlike Lamarck, he worked in the modern episteme (dominant from around 1800), which, in sharp contrast to the Classical episteme, regarded life forms as essentially historical entities and so allowed the possibility of their formation through historical, evolutionary causes. Cuvier, therefore, contradicts Darwin only on the superficial level of what in fact actually happened. Lamarck, although he subscribes to verbal formulas similar to Darwin's, disagrees at a deeper level about what it means to be a species. Between the middle of the 18th century and the middle of the 19th century, there occurred a fundamental break in the European conception of living things; Lamarck was on one side of this division, Cuvier and Darwin on the other. Standard history of ideas misses this key point because it attends only to the theories of individual thinkers and ignores the underlying archaeological frameworks necessary to grasp their ultimate significance.

Foucault provides a detailed formulation of archaeology as a historiographic method in *The Archaeology of Knowledge*, but the method was gradually developed earlier in three histories written in the 1960s: *The History of Madness, The Birth of the Clinic,* and *The Order of Things.* Since it was forged in efforts to treat particular historical problems, it is better evaluated by its historical results than by its persuasiveness as a general epistemological theory. And there have been quite severe assessments by academic historians. Andrew Scull, for example, endorses what he rightly says is 'the verdict of most Anglo-American specialists: that [*The History of Madness*] is a provocative and dazzlingly written prose poem, but one resting on the shakiest of scholarly foundations and riddled with errors of fact and interpretation'.

To illustrate the problems historians have had with Foucault's archaeology, let us take a look at one of his key claims in *The History of Madness:* that, in the middle of the 17th century, the practice of confinement (isolating the mad from the general population in special houses of internment) took on a central significance. According to Foucault, this significance was essentially connected with the Classical Age's fundamental view of madness as a rejection of reason that left no place for the mad in rational society. Roy Porter, until his death in 2002 the leading historian of insanity in the English-speaking world, noted that studies of the treatment of the mad in particular regions of England show 'that lunatics typically remained at large, the responsibility of their family under the eye of the parish'. Although some of the mad were confined, the numbers were quite small: perhaps as few as 5,000 and surely no more than 10,000 by the early 19th century. Confinement, Porter suggests, was much more a 19th-century phenomenon; during the Classical Age, 'the growth in the practice of excluding the mad was gradual, localized, and piecemeal' ('Foucault's Great Confinement', 48).

But notice that Porter's critique is based on just the sort of individual beliefs and actions that are precisely not the primary concern of Foucault's archaeology. Foucault is not making empirical generalizations about what people in various countries thought or did; he is trying to construct the general mode of thinking (episteme) that lay behind what was no doubt a very diverse range of beliefs and practices. An episteme must, admittedly, be reflected in the factual beliefs and actions of those whose thought is constrained by it. But there is no simple correspondence between a general structure of thought and specific beliefs and actions. When my psychoanalyst tells me that I unconsciously hate women, she is not refuted by my truthful claim that I call my mother every week and never forget my wedding anniversary. It may still be true that I have a deep animus toward women that comes out in certain paradigm cases of my behaviour.

Similarly, confinement—whatever the details about its extent in different regions at different times—may represent a distinctive Classical way of thinking about madness. This is not to say that Foucault's claim in unfalsifiable. But it needs to be tested as a general interpretative hypothesis; that is, evaluated by its fruitfulness in making overall sense of a large body of data and suggesting new lines of enquiry. It should not be judged as an empirical generalization—like 'all crows are black'—that can be refuted by a single counter-example.

We may, finally, wonder whether archaeology has any connection with the political orientation of Foucault's work, which we discussed in Chapter 3. It might seem that archaeology, with its emphasis on abstract linguistic structures, could have little to do with the realities of political power, which, admittedly, becomes an explicit theme in Foucault's work only in the 1970s, when he develops his genealogical method. But archaeology is not without its own political (and ethical) potency. This potency arises from its ability to present us with alternative modes of thinking that challenge the necessity that we find in our own modes of thought. Here it is important that Foucault's archaeological analyses are never of cultures radically foreign to ours. He begins *The Order of Things* with the famous quotation from Borges of a categorization, from a mythical 'Chinese encyclopedia', of the types of animals ('belonging to the Emperor', 'embalmed', 'stray dogs', 'included in the present classification', 'innumerable', 'that from a long way off look like flies'). This quotation well represents our reaction when archaeology presents us with a sharply different fundamental mode of thinking: 'the stark impossibility of thinking *that*' (OT, xv). But, while Foucault's archaeologies do exhibit such impossibilities, these are drawn not from the inaccessible distance of a mythical China but from the relatively recent past of our own Western culture: the Europe of the 16th through 18th centuries.

Archaeology, then, shows us apparently 'impossible' modes of thought that were, nonetheless, quite possible for our not so distant intellectual ancestors. We believe, for example, that there is no rational alternative to thinking of madness as 'mental illness', but Foucault's archaeology shows that little more than 200 years ago people such as Descartes and Leibniz—the 'fathers' of our modern scientific world—thought of madness in an entirely different way. Such an exhibition has an implicitly destabilizing effect, suggesting that the framework underlying our concepts and beliefs may not have the inevitability we casually assign it. When these concepts are ones at the basis of ethically and politically charged practices (such as our treatment of the insane, our system of medical practice, our modern social sciences—the subjects, respectively, of Foucault's three archaeological studies), then clearly archaeology is not just a neutral description of linguistic abstractions.

Chapter 5
Genealogy

Since in Foucault's use the term genealogy proclaims his connection to Nietzsche, we should from the first be aware of what Foucault meant by being 'Nietzschean':

> I am tired of people studying [Nietzsche] only to produce the same kind of commentaries that are written on Hegel or Mallarmé. For myself, I prefer to utilise the writers I like. The only valid tribute to a thought such as Nietzsche's is precisely to use it, to deform it, to make it groan and protest. And if commentators then say that I am being faithful or unfaithful to Nietzsche, that is of absolutely no importance.

(P/K, 'Prison Talk', 53–4)

Despite this unequivocal statement, commentators on Foucault have generally assumed that his notion of a genealogy is much the same as Nietzsche's and, in particular, that Foucault's close textual analysis of Nietzsche's notion in 'Nietzsche, Genealogy, History' is a definitive expression of his own view of what genealogy is as a historical methodology.

But this essay was written for a memorial volume in honour of Jean Hyppolite, Foucault's teacher at the École Normale, and is cast, with elegant modesty, as a meticulous *explication de texte*, of the sort Foucault no doubt frequently wrote for his old master. The essay scrupulously summarizes Nietzsche's view of genealogy but seldom comments in Foucault's own voice about the validity of the view. For this reason, we cannot simply assume—as many critics and commentators have—that Foucault himself endorses every formulation of this essay. In some respects, it is clear that the position Foucault presents is not his own. He would not, for example, agree with Nietzsche's frequent references to the feelings and intentions of subjects (the rivalries of scholars, the inventions of the ruling class, 'Nietzsche, Genealogy, History', EW II, 371) as primary engines of the history of thought; nor with Nietzsche's claim that the degeneracy of the 19th century is due to racial mixing (EW II, 384).

Moreover, as I will argue later, it is always risky to take Foucault's general theorizings—about historical method or anything else—as more than tools for some specific purpose. In any case, there is no genealogical counterpart to the detailed retrospective methodological analysis offered in *The Archaeology of Knowledge*. So it makes particular sense to approach genealogy primarily through Foucault's historical practice, not his scattered and not always consistent methodological pronouncements. Taking this approach, the first thing we notice is that there is only one clear sustained use of the genealogical method in Foucault's writings: his history of the prison, *Discipline and Punish*. The first volume of his *History of Sexuality* is ordinarily cited as another genealogical study, but we need to remember that this is merely a general introduction to a series of detailed genealogical studies that were never completed; HS itself offers only a few sketches of what these full studies might have been like. Foucault also sometimes refers to his last two books, on ancient sexuality, as genealogies, but, as we will see, this is so only in a very attenuated sense that has much more to do with their ethical intent than with their mode of historical analysis.

What, then, is the historical methodology of *Discipline and Punish*? The first thing we should notice is the important extent to which the methodology is still archaeological. For example, Foucault presents the distinctively modern technique of punishment by imprisonment in terms of the four main categories of archaeological analysis that he distinguished in *The Archaeology of Knowledge*. Imprisonment constitutes delinquents as a new class of *objects,* characterized by the *concepts* distinctive of the criminal character; moreover, it distinguishes various *modes of authority* (that of the judge, of the parole board, of the criminologist) and alternative *lines of strategic action* (for example, different ways of using solitude and work in the treatment of prisoners). However, the four key archaeological categories are here applied not just to language but also to practices that go beyond mere linguistic expression to produce physical changes in their objects. *Discipline and Punish* is concerned, therefore, not just with the language (analysed by archaeology) through which we know the world, but with the power that changes the world.

Although archaeology is quite capable of describing the conceptual system underlying a practice, linguistic or not, it is not suited to describe the effects of a practice. It is a structural, synchronic mode of analysis, not a causal, diachronic method. Foucault discusses this limitation in his Foreword to the English translation of *The Order of Things*, where he notes that he has restricted himself to a *description* of systems of thought, with no attempt to *explain* changes from one system to another. 'The traditional explanations—spirit of the time, technological or social influences of various kinds—struck me for the most part as being more magical than effective.' However, Foucault had at this point no alternative sort of explanation to offer and so thought 'it would not be prudent... to force a solution I felt incapable, I admit, of offering'. 'Consequently', he says, 'I left the problem of causes to one side; I chose instead to confine myself to describing the transformations themselves, thinking that this would be an indispensable step if, one day, a theory of scientific change and epistemological causality was to be constructed' (OT, xiii).

By the time he wrote *Discipline and Punish*, Foucault had what he saw as an adequate method of causal explanation to complement archaeology. This was what he called genealogy: 'this book is intended...as a genealogy of the present scientific-legal complex' (DP, 23). What had he discovered since writing *The Order of Things?*

The first discovery was that changes in thought are not themselves the products of thought. This corresponds to Foucault's earlier rejection of the 'spirit of the time' and similar quasi-Hegelian modes of historical explanation, such as a collective unconscious. But neither was Foucault happy with historians' standard material modes of explanation in terms of technological or social influences. These are typically vague and general causes—the invention of printing, the rise of the bourgeoisie—that have explanatory force only to the extent that we see history as moving towards correspondingly vague and general goals, such as democracy and secularism. Foucault was sceptical of grand teleological narratives focused on such goals and proposed instead accounts based on many specific 'little' causes, operating independently of one another, with no overall outcome in view. On such an approach we might, for example, discuss not the 'invention of printing' but an entire complex of developments in the production and distribution of newspapers and magazines (new sorts of presses, styles of reporting, methods of making paper, subscription schemes, and so on) that would in turn have a wide and disparate range of social, economic, and political effects. Or, to cite an example from Foucault himself, in *Discipline and Punish* he shows how, among many other things, the invention of a new kind of rifle, more efficient ways of organizing the space of hospitals, and changes in the methods of teaching children penmanship all unwittingly contributed to the formation of a radically new system of social control.

A final discovery: that the objects of these diverse and specific causes are human bodies. The forces that drive our history do not so much operate on our thoughts, our social institutions, or even our environment as on our individual bodies. So, for example, punishment in the 18th century is a matter of violent assaults on the body: branding, dismemberment, execution, whereas in the 19th century it takes the apparently gentler but equally physical form of incarceration, ordered assemblies, and forced labour. Prisoners are subjected to a highly structured regimen designed to produce 'docile bodies'. A Foucaultian genealogy, then, is a historical causal explanation that is material, multiple, and corporeal.

Is it then Nietzschean? Nietzsche (like Foucault himself) offers many programmatic remarks on genealogy—not all mutually consistent—among which can be found passages that match the main elements of Foucault's practice. For example, Nietzsche (Figure 6) speaks of genealogy in terms of tracing the *Herkunft* (stock or descent) of an idea or practice, which connects with Foucault's emphasis on the body. Similarly, Nietzsche presents genealogy as naturalistic rather than idealistic and talks of explaining morality, in particular, as a contingent phenomenon that developed from small 'accidental' causes. In fact, however, Nietzsche's most worked-out genealogy *(The Genealogy of Morality)* is very different from the project Foucault undertakes in *Discipline and Punish*. For one thing, Nietzsche's effort has nothing of the careful scholarship and documentary detail of Foucault's book. It is not the product of serious archival research—'gray, meticulous, and patiently documentary' ('Nietzsche, Genealogy, History', EW II, 369)—but of an erudite amateur's armchair speculations. More significantly, Nietzsche's genealogy operates with psychological causes (the pride and

6. 'The Holy Trinity': Lou Salomé, Paul Rée, and Friedrich Nietzsche, May 1882.

ambition of the strong, the resentment of the weak, the malicious ingenuity of priests), which have little to do with Foucault's history of the body. Foucault offers no parallels to Nietzsche's deployment of Socratic weakness and Pauline rancour as key genealogical causes. Further, Christianity—the primary source, in Nietzsche's account, of what we mean by morality—is a global and monolithic cause, relentlessly insisting on the renunciation of this world in favour of an 'afterlife'. Simply as historical methodologies, Nietzsche's and Foucault's genealogies are quite different.

Nonetheless, Foucault is thoroughly Nietzschean in one fundamental respect: the critical intent with which he employs his genealogy. Nietzsche used genealogy to show that our most revered institutions and practices were 'human, all-too-human'. Foucault's genealogies likewise deconstruct, by showing their real origin, official meanings and evaluations involved in a society's self-understanding. 'Historical beginnings are lowly: not in the sense of modest or discreet like the steps of a dove, but derisive and ironic, capable of undoing every infatuation' (EW II, 372). To provide a genealogy is 'to identify the accidents, the minute deviations—or, conversely, the complete reversals—the errors, the false appraisals, and the faulty calculations that give birth to those things that continue to exist and have value for us' (EW II, 374). These quotations are Foucault's exposition of Nietzsche, but in this case they speak for himself as well.

It may seem that this critical use of genealogy falls into the genetic fallacy, arguing from the lowly origin of something to its lack of value. Suppose Nietzsche is right that morality originates 'in detestable, narrow-minded conclusions. *Pudenda origo* [shameful origin]' (*Dawn*, #102; cited in EW II, 370). How does that prove that morality has no authority? Or why, as Nietzsche also suggests, should our evolution from 'lower' animals undermine human dignity: 'We wished to awaken the feeling of man's sovereignty by showing his divine birth; this path is now forbidden, since a monkey stands at the entrance' (*Dawn*, #49; cited in EW II, 372).

It is not, however, the genealogist who introduces the question of origins. This is done when, for example, the Ten Commandments are said to have moral authority because God handed them to Moses on Mount Sinai, or when the subordination of women is said to be required by their biological nature. The fact of evolution does not refute human dignity, but it may help undermine, as the quote above from Nietzsche suggests, the claim that this dignity is grounded in our direct creation by God. Genealogical critique will avoid the genetic fallacy as long as it is directed at efforts to support established authorities on the basis of their origin. This understanding of genealogy is implicit in Foucault's claim that it reveals the contingency of that which was said to be necessary. Here necessity (due to divine will, human nature, or transcendental conditions of possibility) is the general category under which fall all efforts to justify practices and institutions in terms of their privileged origin.

Foucault sums up the value-orientation of genealogy by saying that it is a 'history of the present' (DP, 30–1). This is so in two senses. First, the subject matter of the history is the origins of present rules, practices, or institutions that claim an authority over us. Second, the primary intent is not to understand the past in its own terms or for its own sake, but to understand and evaluate the present, particularly with a view to discrediting unjustified claims of authority. As a proponent of the idea of a history of the present, Foucault stands firmly with Nietzsche, however much the claim that their historical methods are the same must 'distort' Nietzsche's own practice, and 'make it groan and protest'.

There is another crucial area where Foucault's genealogy obviously evokes Nietzsche: in its claim that there is an intimate tie between knowledge and power. This claim develops Foucault's basic insight that changes in thought are not due to thought itself, suggesting that when thoughts change the causes are the social forces that control the behaviour of individuals. Specifically, given Foucault's archaeological view of knowledge, power transforms the fundamental archaeological frameworks (epistemes or discursive formations) that underlie our knowledge. Foucault is here staking out a position between the extremes of reducing knowledge to power (that is, the identification of 'A knows that p' with 'social forces compel A to accept p') and asserting the essential independence of knowledge and power (that is, the Utopian claim that 'A knows that p' implies 'A's acceptance of p is causally independent of all social forces'). To know is not simply to be affected by power; as Foucault once said of power and knowledge, 'The very fact that I pose the question of their relation proves clearly that I do not *identify* them' ('Critical Theory/Intellectual History', 43). On the other hand, knowing does not involve a total escape from power relations.

Moreover, Foucault claims that power has a positive epistemic role, not only constraining or eliminating knowledge but also producing it. Classical economics, for example, is a product of the capitalist socio-economic system that, despite obvious limitations due to its origin, has achieved a distinctive body of knowledge that would not exist without capitalism (AK, 186). Further, knowledge can have a transforming effect on the power structures that give rise to it. For example, governments that claim justification on the basis of a given body of knowledge (for example, of a people's history) can be challenged on the basis of those facts. Think of the political significance in Israel of new archaeological findings that can be interpreted as supporting or undermining Biblical claims about the early Judaic nation.

The idea that power and knowledge are closely bound readily recalls Nietzsche's obscure and controversial conception of the will-to-power, which he presents as the source of systems of thought (for example, Platonic philosophy, Christian theology) that claim to express pure, objective knowledge. Foucault had no sympathy for the metaphysical theorizing that is sometimes the context of Nietzsche's talk of will-to-power. But he was clearly

49

impressed by and adopted Nietzsche's technique of looking for power behind sciences, religions, and other cognitive authorities that present themselves as grounded in nothing more than the force of disinterested evidence and argument.

It is less clear that Foucault owes very much to Nietzsche for his idea that power can be productive of genuine knowledge. 'Nietzsche, Genealogy, History', at least, considers only the negative results of Nietzschean genealogy. Power for Nietzsche, as Foucault reads him, is always violence. Humans do establish systems of rules (social and, presumably, also epistemic), but these are merely vehicles for violent domination:

> Humanity does not gradually progress from combat to combat until it arrives at universal reciprocity, where the rule of law finally replaces warfare; humanity installs each of its violences in a system of rules and thus proceeds from domination to domination.

Interpretation, certainly an essential part of any system of knowledge, is for Foucault's Nietzsche 'the violent or surreptitious appropriation of a system of rules ... in order to impose a direction, to bend it to a new will, to force its participation in a new game' (EW II, 378). It is hard to see how power that expresses itself exclusively in violence and domination can produce knowledge.

On the other hand, we may find it implausible to think that power can ever produce knowledge. Such doubt underlies the persistent claim (sometimes presented as criticism, sometimes as plaudit) that Foucault leaves no room for objective, non-relativized truth. If, the thought goes, everything I believe is determined by the power structures of my society, how can any of my beliefs have validity except relative to the standards of that society? And, although there are some who praise Foucault for jettisoning outdated and repressive notions of objective truth, there seems to be much more point to the critics' argument that such a position is self-refuting. If all beliefs are valid only relative to the power system from which they originate, then Foucault's relativist claims themselves have at best only this restricted validity. If we are subject to the same power regime as Foucault, presumably we already accept his position. If we are not, it has no relevance to us.

But why think that power cannot produce genuine knowledge? Of course, there are familiar cases such as brainwashing in which the causal production of belief by power relations negates the very possibility of knowledge. If you have forced me, through sleep deprivation and sensory disorientation, to believe that the Party's aims are good, then I cannot be said to know this, even if it happens to be true. But this does not mean that there are no forms of training and guidance (education, we might call it) that can produce genuine knowledge. Surely this is how children are initiated into the rudiments of mathematical, historical, and moral knowledge. As we grow up, a certain amount of what we have been taught becomes subject to reflective assessment, but certainly much of what we believe remains the result of social conditioning. Such examples, of course, are on the level of the conscious knowledge of individuals (*connaissance*, in Foucault's terminology), whereas Foucault is concerned with the underlying archaeological structures of knowledge (*savoir*). But the principle is the same in both cases: the mere fact that a cognitive state is an effect of power does not exclude it from the realm of knowledge. Power and knowledge are logically compatible.

Whatever we may think of this general defence, it is not clear that Foucault really needs it. He is, in the end, not interested in the sort of theoretical generalizations that lead to radical relativism and scepticism. Despite occasional unguarded universal claims, he is only committed to regional, not global, scepticism. His project is to question quite specific claims to cognitive authority: roughly, those made by psychologists and social scientists (and not even all such claims). He clearly has no problem with many other domains, such as mathematics, physics, chemistry, and much of biology. His genealogies, therefore, should present particular reasons why we should doubt the claims to cognitive authority made by specific disciplines, not reasons to doubt any such claim at all. They should show that there is something particularly wrong with psychiatry or criminology that makes it a 'dubious discipline'. As we will soon see, this is precisely what his genealogies do.

Chapter 6
The masked philosopher

Typically elusive regarding identity, Foucault sometimes allows and sometimes denies that he is a philosopher. When he consented to an interview in a series presenting the views of 'philosophers', he insisted on anonymity, presenting himself as a 'masked philosopher' ('The Masked Philosopher', EW I, 321–8).

The bureaucrats were quite certain that Foucault was a philosopher. He possessed advanced degrees in the subject (including the highest level, the *doctorat d'état*) and was a professor in several philosophy departments. Why, then, his own—and our—ambivalence?

To find an interesting answer to the question 'is X a philosopher?', we need a relevant context, which is most easily supplied by paradigm examples of philosophical activity. Is Foucault a philosopher in the sense of Socrates drinking the hemlock, of Diogenes searching with his lamp, of Descartes meditating in his room? In our time, the paradigm is Kant, who established philosophy as an autonomous theoretical enterprise: not, as for the ancients, a life-guiding wisdom; nor, as for the medievals, a handmaid to theology; nor even, as for Descartes and other early moderns, as part of a new scientific account of the world. In Kant—at least as the author of his three great critiques—philosophy presents itself as an academic discipline, alongside other disciplines, such as physics and mathematics, with its own theoretical goals, methods, and domain of enquiry. As a result, philosophy became a technical, specialist subject, not accessible to even highly educated non-professionals. Lord Macaulay, for example, complained that he, who had no problem with Plato, Descartes, or Hume, simply could not read Kant's *Critique of Pure Reason* (a book that, as Richard Rorty has said, anyone who is a philosopher must have read).

So, we might well ask, is Foucault a philosopher in this modern Kantian sense? The bureaucrats' criteria tell us that, at least, he was trained and certified as a philosopher in this sense. But was his work actually a contribution to the modern (Kantian) philosophical project?

Here we can turn to Foucault's own discussion of Kant and modern philosophy in an essay, published the year he died (1984), entitled 'What is Enlightenment?'. Quite typically, Foucault does not take as his touchstone Kant's 'major' works, such as the three critiques, but a short essay, 'a minor text, perhaps' (EW III, 303), that Kant also called 'Was ist Aufklärung?'. Foucault begins this essay with the suggestion that modern philosophy may well be defined as the effort to answer Kant's question: 'What is Enlightenment?'.

But what does this question mean? The Enlightenment was a distinctively modern movement, directed towards using reason to free mankind from the constraints imposed by traditional authorities—intellectual, religious, and political. In his essay, Kant said that the point of Enlightenment was to overcome our 'immaturity' by daring to think for ourselves (*sapere aude*), rather than accepting the authority of others. Foucault summarizes Kant's three examples: 'we are in a state of "immaturity" when a book takes the place of our understanding, when a spiritual director takes the place of our conscience, and when a doctor decides for us what our diet is to be' (EW III, 305).

Thinking for ourselves means reasoning: 'Kant, in fact, describes Enlightenment as the moment when humanity is going to put its own reason to use, without subjecting itself to any authority'. Kant understands his own philosophical project of the critique of reason as a necessary precondition of Enlightenment: 'it is precisely at this moment that the critique is necessary, since its role is that of defining the conditions under which the use of reason is legitimate' (EW III, 308); that is, the conditions that limit the proper employment of reason. Kant, for example, argued in his First Critique that theoretical reason could not be legitimately applied to 'limit-questions' such as the origin of the universe or the immortality of the soul.

But what Foucault finds distinctive and important about Kant's discussion of Enlightenment is not the details of his critique of reason but the fact that he is reflecting on 'the contemporary status of his own enterprise' (EW III, 309). Nor is the question how contemporary philosophy fits into the general scheme of history (for example, as herald of a bright new future or a falling away from a golden age). The question is simply what makes our present way of doing philosophy different from what was done previously. This, Foucault maintains, is a new and important development: to focus philosophy not on perennial questions but on the question of what is distinctive about our current situation.

So, then, what is distinctive about our current situation? To answer this question, Foucault redirects his discussion from Kant on Enlightenment to Baudelaire on modernity. In one sense, this is simply a move to a new terminology—Enlightenment being the distinctive feature of the modern age—and to a new example, Baudelaire's aesthetic rather than Kant's moral and political perspective. But in fact the shift reflects what Foucault sees as some crucial differences between our situation and Kant's. Our (Baudelairean) modernity is a historical development from Kant's Enlightenment, but one that has substantively transformed it.

Accordingly, just as Kant (in 'Was ist Aufklärung?') asks how his situation is different from that of his predecessors, so Foucault asks how his situation is different from Kant's.

To begin with, we cannot follow Kant in thinking that the critique of reason discovers essential and universal (transcendental) truths that mark the limits of human experience and thought. On Foucault's reading, Baudelaire's modernity is an attitude that finds something 'eternally' valuable in the present moment, while, at the same time, striving to transform it 'not by destroying it but by grasping it in what it is'. 'Baudelairean modernity is an exercise in which extreme attention to what is real is confronted with the practice of a liberty that simultaneously respects this reality and violates it' (EW III, 311). Here we should think of the tender exactness of, say, Courbet's rendering of a mundane moment, which simultaneously preserves and transforms it. Moreover, this modern project of transformation applies above all to the self:

> to be modern is not to accept oneself as one is in the flux of the
> passing moments; it is to take oneself as object of a complex and
> difficult elaboration…Modern man, for Baudelaire, is not the man
> who goes off to discover himself, his secrets and his hidden truth;
> he is the man who tries to invent himself.

(EW III, 311)

Foucault clearly does not accept all the details of Baudelaire's picture of modernity, for example, his understanding of self-transformation in terms of the dandy's anti-natural elegance, or his claim that the modern project cannot be carried out politically or socially but only aesthetically. But Foucault does accept a general 'ethos' of modernity, which, he says, consists not in any set of doctrines but in a critical attitude or orientation towards our historical era. Further, this orientation is, like Baudelaire's, towards a transformation of the present self.

Now we can return to Foucault's relation to Kant's philosophical project. He accepts the general Enlightenment goal of critique but reverses its polarity:

> Criticism indeed consists of analyzing and reflecting upon limits. But if the Kantian question was that of knowing [*savoir*] what limits knowledge [*connaissance*] must renounce exceeding, it seems to me that the critical question today must be turned back into a positive one: In what is given to us as universal, necessary, obligatory, what place is occupied by whatever is singular, contingent, and the product of arbitrary constraints?
>
> (EW III, 315)

This key passage formulates Foucault's final conception of his enterprise as one of philosophical critique. In Kant's terminology, it is *critical* (examining assumptions regarding the scope and limits of our knowledge), but it is not, like Kant's own project, *transcendental*. It does not, that is, claim to discover necessary conditions for knowing that determine categories in terms of which we must experience and think about the world and ourselves. Rather, Foucault's critique examines claims of necessity with a view to undermining them by showing that they are merely historical contingencies. Referring to his earlier methodological discussions, he says that his project is 'not transcendental' but 'genealogical in its design and archaeological in its method'. Its method is 'archaeological—and not transcendental—in the sense that it will not seek to identify the universal structures of all knowledge [*connaissance*] or of all possible moral action, but will seek to treat the instances of discourse that articulate what we think, say, and do as so many historical events' (EW III, 315). Similarly, Foucault's project is genealogical because it is not designed to discover 'what is impossible for us to do or to know', but to uncover 'the possibility of no longer being, doing, or thinking what we are, do, or think' (EW III, 315–16).

57

So in the Kantian terms that define the modern idea of philosophy, Foucault is a philosopher to the extent that he shares the general critical orientation of the philosophical project. But he does not share the interest of Kant—and of most other modern philosophers—in finding a distinctive realm of philosophical truth that delimits necessary conditions on thought, experience, and action. He is not, for example, interested in phenomenological intuitions of essences, or in the necessary and sufficient conditions sought by linguistic analysis. His interest is rather in the uncovering of possibilities that intuition and analysis might well claim do not exist. There is no reason that Foucault need deny that the phenomenological or linguistic analysis might reveal genuinely necessary, universal truths. But his philosophical project is directed not towards such truths but towards contingencies masked as necessities. In addition, the methods he uses—archaeology and genealogy—are, as we have seen, methods of historical investigation, not of a priori philosophical analysis. In Kantian terms, he is a philosopher only in his generic commitment to critique, not in his specific understanding of, nor in his methods of carrying out, his critical project.

We might, therefore, be inclined to conclude that Foucault is not a philosopher in any substantive sense—except for the fact that philosophy after Kant has itself involved a continuing critique of its own project. In most cases—from German idealism through analytic philosophy—the enterprise has remained broadly Kantian. Foucault, like Nietzsche, pushes this critique to an extreme, since he rejects the ideal of philosophy as a body of autonomous truths. But if this critical direction continues and eventually triumphs, then Foucault may well be hailed as a founder of a new mode of philosophy. It would surely not displease Foucault to think that the answer to the question 'is X a philosopher?' will depend on the future history of philosophy.

Regardless of how we decide to classify him, there is no doubt that Foucault emerged from a philosophical context and that his writings often impinge on philosophical issues. He formulated succinctly the philosophical context: 'I belong to that generation who as students had before their eyes, and were limited by, a horizon consisting of Marxism, phenomenology, and existentialism' (RR, interview, 174). We have already seen Foucault's early disillusion with Marxism. The ties to phenomenology and existentialism were more enduring, but quite complex. Foucault had studied with Merleau-Ponty, who, along with Sartre, was the leading figure in the appropriation of Husserl's phenomenology by the French existentialists, and with Jean Hyppolite, a major Hegel scholar with a strong interest in existentialism. Heidegger's *Being and Time* was also very important for the young Foucault, who was also especially interested in the Heideggerian existential psychiatry (*Daseinanalysis*) of Ludwig Binswanger.

Whatever the exact nature of Foucault's early commitment to existential phenomenology, there is no doubt that he rather soon decided that the subjective standpoint of phenomenological description was not adequate. But his path away from existential phenomenology is not entirely clear. In general, phenomenology declined in the 1960s in the wake of the spectacular rise of what was called 'structuralism', a set of diversely developed theoretical standpoints, all of which explained human phenomena in terms of underlying unconscious structures rather than the lived experience described by phenomenology. There were, for example, Saussure's linguistics, Lacan's psychoanalysis, the literary criticism of Roland Barthes, the anthropology of Claude Lévi-Strauss, and Georges Dumézil's comparative studies of the structures of ancient religions. Foucault always denied that he was a structuralist and ridiculed his assimilation to the movement by the middle-brow intellectual media. (He had described his approach as 'structural' at various points in *The Birth of the Clinic* but pointedly eliminated the word in later printings.) Since structuralism was an avowedly non-historical (synchronic rather than diachronic) approach, there was point to Foucault's protest. But there are obvious affinities between structuralist theories and Foucault's archaeology (he particularly emphasizes the significance for him of Dumézil's work); and he cites the inadequacy of phenomenology's accounts of language and the unconscious, in comparison to structuralist accounts, as a good reason for its decline.

But there were also more distinctive features of Foucault's thinking that turned him away from phenomenology. For example, he emphasized the importance of avant-garde literature's decentring of the author and the psychological subject, and said that his reading of Nietzsche (around 1953, inspired by Bataille and Blanchot, well before Nietzsche became fashionable in France) played an important role in his break with subject-centred philosophy (interview, 'Structuralism and Poststructuralism', EW II, 439). However, the most important factor was Foucault's association with French history and philosophy of science, particularly as practised by Georges Canguilhem, who was the official director of Foucault's thesis on the history of madness.

On Foucault's own account, Canguilhem (along with his predecessor at the Sorbonne, Gaston Bachelard) represented a clear alternative to phenomenology, one that emphasized the logic of concepts rather than lived experience as the driving force in human thought. Canguilhem's students—among whom Foucault explicitly placed himself—rejected phenomenology's 'philosophy of experience' in favour of Canguilhem's 'philosophy of the concept'. Canguilhem's histories of concepts were important models for Foucault's archaeologies of the 1960s. Years later, in an essay on Canguilhem ('Life: Experience and Science', EW II, 465–78), Foucault sketched a biological conception of experience designed to replace the subject-centred phenomenological *vécu* (lived experience).

But, at least for Foucault, the tradition of Bachelard (Figure 7) and Canguilhem provided more a methodological alternative to phenomenology than a philosophical critique of it. For such a

7. Gaston Bachelard.

critique we must turn to Foucault's study of modern thought in *The Order of Things*. The ultimate purpose of this book was to understand the archaeological framework (episteme) underlying the modern social sciences, but, since Foucault thinks this framework is dominated by the philosophical concept of 'man', particularly associated with Kant, his discussion includes a critical history of modern philosophy.

From Descartes on, modern philosophy has been preoccupied with the question of whether our representations (experiences, ideas) accurately represent the world outside our minds. Descartes, for example, asked how we know that our ideas correspond to things that actually exist outside of us in space and time. Hume asked how we know that our experiences of regular associations of ideas (for example, the sun rising each new day) correspond to necessary connections in reality. Until Kant, no one had a plausible answer to these questions (though there were some persuasive suggestions, from Hume for example, that they needed no answer).

With Kant there occurred a decisive turn because he also reflected on the very possibility of representation, asking not just whether our representations are true to the world but how it is possible that we can represent anything at all (accurately or not). This was decisive because, he maintained, answering the new question provided a way of answering the old one. In particular, Kant argued that the very possibility of representing an object at all required, for example, that the object be represented as existing in space and time and as part of a network of causal laws. According to this kind of argument (which Kant called a 'transcendental deduction'), the objects of our experience exist in space and time and are governed by necessary causal laws because otherwise they could not be objects of our experience. On the one hand, we are limited to knowing the world as we experience it (the phenomenal world), not the world as it is in itself (the noumenal world). On the other hand, this very limitation makes it possible for us to have objective knowledge of a world.

Kant's view of knowledge requires a special dual status for human beings. On the one hand, we are the source of the necessary conditions for the possibility of any knowledge of the world: we belong to a 'transcendental' domain that is the source of all knowledge in the 'empirical' domain. But at the same time we are ourselves knowable (not only by experience but also by the social sciences) and so are objects in the empirical domain. Foucault uses the term 'man' to refer to human beings as having this peculiar dual status (as what he calls an 'empirical-transcendental doublet'). He argues that, in this sense, there was no conception of man prior to the end of the 18th century. Hence his melodramatic declaration that, until the 19th century, *'man* did not exist' (OT, 308).

In Foucault's history of modern philosophy, man is the central problem, the difficulty being to understand how a single unified being can be simultaneously the transcendental source of the possibility of knowledge and just another object of knowledge. Chapter 9 of *The Order of Things* works through the major developments of 20th-century philosophy—particularly the phenomenologies of Husserl, Sartre, and Merleau-Ponty—arguing that none of them is able to develop a coherent conception of man. In every case, there is an illegitimate reduction: either of the empirical to the transcendental (Husserl) or of the transcendental to the empirical (Merleau-Ponty).

This chapter is the closest the mature Foucault ever comes to standard philosophical discourse in the Kantian mode. It can be plausibly read—as I just have—as an effort to show that all modern explications of man (as an empirical-transcendental doublet) have fallen into incoherence. But such a reading—even though it seems to accord with Foucault's own intentions—falls foul of his archaeological project of *The Order of Things*. For it puts his discussion on the level of history of ideas, the story of a series of individual thinkers trying to resolve a problem, not an archaeological investigation of the unconscious structures subtending such history. Further, as history of ideas, it can only tell us that these particular thinkers have failed to solve their problem, not that there are reasons in principle (presumably at the archaeological level) for the failure. If, however, we reconstrue Foucault's treatment as a genuinely archaeological account, then the apparent incoherence of the concept of man shows nothing more than that our thought is no longer guided by the modern episteme, with the result that we are, like readers of Borges' Chinese encyclopedia, faced with 'the stark impossibility of thinking *that*'. In neither instance has Foucault made an effective case for or against a standard philosophical position. Nor is that, on his own account, surprising, since making such a case would require Foucault to operate within the modern episteme itself (the framework of philosophy in the Kantian sense), thereby giving up the historical distance required by his archaeological methodology. I conclude, then, that even in his most apparently philosophical moments, Foucault is not a participant in the debates of modern post-Kantian philosophy.

There remains, however, a further possibility, one that has attracted some readers of *The Order of Things*. This is that Foucault, following Heidegger, is trying to open a path to a new mode of philosophical thinking that will take us beyond the modern episteme. There are certainly Heideggerian elements in *The Order of Things*. Most prominent is the very critique of representation and of the philosophy of experience, which distinctly evokes a main theme of *Being and Time*; and, if Foucault suggests that Heidegger himself does not escape from the representationalist picture, that is a standard move in Heideggerian critiques of the master. There are also ruminations about the relation of language to being that surely have Heidegger's later writings in mind: 'What relation is there between language and being, and is it really to being that language is always addressed?' (OT, 306). And the opening and closing attacks on the idea of 'man', with their intimation that we are moving to a new age in which 'humanism' will vanish, seem calculated to put Foucault on Heidegger's side in his famous attack on Sartre in the 'Letter on Humanism'.

But these Heideggerian features are just what separate *The Order of Things* from the rest of Foucault's books. Nowhere else are philosophical themes so prominent, nowhere else is there so little connection of the discussion with the ethical and political issues characteristic of a 'history of the present'. Although written as an archaeology of the social sciences, it is extremely difficult to connect its analysis with the system of domination in which these disciplines are, as Foucault's later work shows, so closely implicated. The idea of 'man' may be an arbitrary constraint on our thought, but we have no sense that going beyond it will be anything more than an exercise in intellectual freedom. It is also worth remembering that large portions of *The Order of Things* are quite non-Heideggerian, particularly in their meticulous concern with the details of scientific modes of thought. But to the extent that the book is Heideggerian, it demonstrates that his other books are not.

Chapter 7
Madness

For us, 'mad' and 'mentally ill' are synonyms. We know that the sorts of people who cannot stop shouting obscenities at strangers or who think they receive radio messages from Pluto via their dental fillings have not always been regarded as suffering from an illness. They were said to be possessed by a god, in league with the devil, or simply subhuman animals. But we think that alternative views of madness are signs of ignorance if not malice; they lost all intellectual respectability after our modern discovery that madness is mental illness.

Standard histories of psychiatry have canonized this view. During the French Revolution, Philippe Pinel (Figure 8) protested against chaining the mad like animals and went to the house of confinement at Bicêtre to release them. There he was confronted by Courthon, a fanatical member of the Republican government, who objected. Foucault quotes the story (MC, 242) with predictable irony:

> Turning to Pinel [Courthon said]: 'Now, citizen, are you mad yourself to seek to unchain such beasts?' Pinel replied calmly: 'Citizen, I am convinced that these madmen are so intractable only because they have been deprived of air and liberty.' 'Well, do as you like with them, but I fear you may become the victim of your own presumption.' Whereupon, Couthon was taken to his

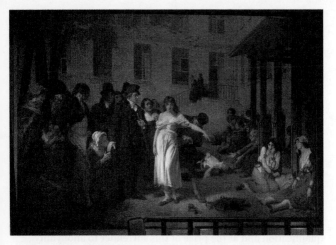

8. *Pinel Freeing the Insane* (1876), oil painting by Tony Robert-Fleury, Salpêtrière Hospital, Paris.

carriage...Everyone breathed again; the great philanthropist immediately set to work.

Such stories—there are similar ones about Samuel Tuke, who founded a Quaker asylum (the 'Retreat') in England about the same time—portray their heroes as brave and compassionate men who rejected superstitions in favour of scientifically based treatment of what enlightened thought showed to be an illness. But, Foucault maintains, 'the truth was quite different' (MC, 243).

Tuke's work, for example, had religious and moral, not scientific, motivations. The Retreat freed the mad from chains and physical abuse and placed them in a halcyon setting. But in this setting they were strictly monitored for any deviations from conventional behaviour. The therapy consisted in making the madman 'feel morally responsible for everything in him that may disturb morality and society, and must hold no one but himself responsible' (MC, 246). The upshot was that 'Tuke created an asylum where he

67

substituted for the free terror of madness the stifling anguish of responsibility' (MC, 247).

An exemplary moment in Tuke's treatment was his famous 'tea-parties', 'social occasions in the English manner', Foucault tells us. Here the mad are guests of the directors and staff of the Retreat and (here Foucault quotes Tuke's account) 'vie with each other in politeness and propriety'. Remarkably, 'the evening generally passes with the greatest harmony and enjoyment... and the scene is at once curious and affectingly gratifying' (MC, 249). But Foucault has a very different reading of these occasions: 'The madman is obliged to objectify himself in the eyes of reason as the perfect stranger, that is, the man whose strangeness does not reveal itself. The city of reason welcomes him only with this qualification and at the price of this surrender to anonymity' (MC, 249–50).

Foucault resists the picture of Tuke and Pinel as humanitarians because he rejects their view that 'humanity' entails the values of modern bourgeois society: 'Now the asylum must represent the great continuity of social morality. The values of family and work, all the acknowledged virtues, now reign in the asylum' (MC, 257), which Foucault insists 'is not a free realm of observation, diagnosis, and therapeutics' but 'a juridical space where one is accused, judged and condemned'. The mad are freed from their chains but they are 'imprisoned in a moral world' (MC, 269). There is a 'gigantic moral imprisonment' that, Foucault sneers, 'we are in the habit of calling, doubtless by antiphrasis, the liberation of the insane' (MC, 278).

We may well see something preciously unrealistic in Foucault's sarcasm. After all, the mad are not rebels against a particular social or moral system; they are radically dysfunctional in any meaningful human context. If Tuke's tea-parties help control a psychotic who would otherwise try to kill anyone he met, then why worry that they reinforce bourgeois morality?

Foucault, who had worked with the mad, presumably knew that often a psychotic is just a psychotic, and he would surely have welcomed a treatment that returned delusional murderers to conventional morality. His outrage is directed, rather, against a perception of madness that admits no meaningful alternatives to our standards of normality and puts all belief and behaviour that seriously deviate from these standards outside the pale. On Foucault's view, madness as a general phenomenon should be seen as a creditable challenge to normality, even though there are insane horrors to which normality would be a welcome relief.

But this response on Foucault's behalf assumes that madness might be something besides beyond the pale. Is this really possible? If we don't think so, Foucault says, this is because of the way madness has, historically, come to be perceived by our culture. His *History of Madness* is a sustained argument for this conclusion.

He begins with a cursory but crucial survey of madness in the Middle Ages and the Renaissance. Then, he maintains, madness was seen as an integrally human phenomenon. Madness was opposed to reason, but as an alternative mode of human existence, not a simple rejection of it. Consequently, madness (even if disdained or abhorred) was a meaningful challenge to reason. It could engage in ironic dialogue with reason (as in Erasmus' *In Praise of Folly*) or claim a domain of human experience and insight not available to reason (as in Bosch's paintings or Shakespeare's tragedies). The point, in any case, is that in the past madness had a significant role in our culture's understanding of human possibilities.

This fruitful understanding of madness ended around the middle of the 17th century, just at the beginning of what the French call the Classical Age. In contrast to medieval and Renaissance views, the Classical Age saw madness as merely the negation of the essential human attribute of reason. It was regarded as unreason (*déraison*), a plunge into an animality that had no human significance. There was, accordingly, a *conceptual exclusion* of the mad from the human world. So, for example, Descartes in his First Meditation entertains a range of possibilities as grounds for doubting his beliefs: the senses might be deceptive, he might be dreaming, there might even be an omnipotent evil demon bent on deceiving him at every turn. But, Foucault notes (HF, 56–8), there is one possibility at which Descartes baulks. After suggesting that his beliefs might be unreliable because he is like those who think their heads are pumpkins or made of glass, he immediately rejects the possibility: 'But they are mad, and I would be mad myself if I thought for a moment that I was like them' (Meditation I). (Foucault and Jacques Derrida had a tense debate over the interpretation of this passage.)

Correlative to this conceptual exclusion, there was a physical exclusion of the mad effected by their confinement in institutions that isolated them from ordinary human life. This was most strikingly signalled in France by the 'Great Confinement' of 1656, when, within a period of just a few months, over 1 per cent of the population of Paris was compelled to live in the dispersed sections of the Hôpital Général. (One of these sections was Salpêtrière, today a modern hospital, where—irony of ironies—Foucault himself died in 1984.) But Foucault maintains that similar confinements occurred throughout Europe.

The conceptual and physical exclusion of the mad also reflects a moral condemnation. The moral fault, however, is not the ordinary sort, whereby a member of the human community violates one of its basic norms. Rather, madness corresponds to a radical choice that rejects humanity and the human community *in toto* in favour of a life of sheer (non-human) animality. On the Classical view, the animality of the mad is expressed in their domination by passions, a domination that leads them to a delirium in which they mistake the unreal for the real. Passionate delirium thus results in a fundamental blindness that cuts the mad off from the light of reason.

The modern therapeutic view of madness is a sharp break with the Classical view, what Foucault later calls a change in episteme or discursive formation. The mad are returned to the human community, no longer animals beyond the human pale. But, within that community, the mad are now moral offenders (violators of specific social norms), who should feel guilt at their condition and need reform of their attitudes and behaviour. Correspondingly, the characteristic modern mode of treating the mad not only isolates them but subjects them to a moralizing therapy. Still, this move from the custodial confinement of the Classical Age to the modern therapeutic asylum continues to deny madness as a humanly significant challenge.

We may object that the quite explicit moral orientation of Pinel and Tuke excludes them as founders of modern psychiatry, which is avowedly ethically neutral in treating a disease that is not regarded as the patient's fault. Surely there is a distinction between these early moral therapies and the subsequent medicalization of the treatment of the mad? Foucault's response is that the most striking feature of the moral domination of the asylum was 'the apotheosis of the medical personage' (MC, 269). We, convinced that the mad are simply 'mentally ill', think it inevitable that doctors should control their care. But Foucault claims that, in the asylum, the rule is never so much by medical as by moral authority. Doctors have authority not because they have the knowledge to cure (this is haphazard at best) but because they represent the moral demands of society. This is evident today in psychiatric practice. This wears the trappings of medical science, but the key to therapy remains the personal moral authority of the therapist, who serves as an instrument of social values. Hence, for example, the essential role of transference in psychoanalytic treatment.

Foucault's account seems implausible only if we continue to insist that the identification of madness as mental illness is an objective scientific discovery. His history, however, suggests that the identification was, on the contrary, introduced as a means of legitimizing the authority of physicians in the asylum once the idea of a distinctively moral therapy was abandoned. The fact that physicians came to be in charge of asylums initially had little to do with their medical expertise. The moral treatments recommended by Tuke and Pinel were not essentially medical and could be carried out by any person with moral authority. However, as the 19th century developed, medicine became dominated by the ideal of objective, value-free knowledge, which left no room for value-laden moral therapies. The idea of a distinctively mental sort of illness was introduced primarily to justify the continuing authority of doctors over the mad, not because of its scientific truth or curative success.

But even if contemporary psychiatry falls short of the claims of scientific objectivity it sometimes makes, we might still ask if it really allows no meaningful interaction with the mad. Isn't psychoanalysis an obvious counter-example, since it removes patients from the strictures of the asylum and actually listens to them? Foucault agrees that Freud eliminates most features of the asylum, retaining only the core relation of doctor to patient. But, as we've seen, this relation is at the heart of the modern domination of the mad. Moreover, according to Foucault, Freud 'amplified...the thaumaturgical powers' of the 'medical personage', giving it a 'quasi-divine status' (MC, 277). In the person of the analyst, Freud 'focused...all the powers...of the asylum' (MC, 277–8). The analyst does listen to the patient but, silent behind the couch, is transformed into 'an absolute Observation, a pure and circumspect Silence, a Judge who punishes and rewards in a judgment that does not even condescend to language'. As a result, psychoanalysis 'has not been able, will not be able, to hear the voices of unreason'. It is effective in some cases but, in the end, 'remains a stranger to the sovereign enterprise of unreason' (MC, 278).

But if madness has been silenced, how has Foucault become, as he so obviously is, fascinated by its voice? From the only way in which madness has manifested itself since the end of the 18th century: 'in the lightning-flash of works such as those of Hölderlin, of Nerval, of Nietzsche, or of Artaud' (MC, 278), the great mad artists of the last two centuries. We have already noted the connection between the theme of mad artists and Foucault's interest in avant-garde art. In both cases, his idea is that probing the limits of reason will reveal truths that are not rationally accessible.

This idea reflects a tension that pervades *The History of Madness* and erupts especially at the beginning and the end. In his preface (dropped in the second edition) and in his conclusion, Foucault suggests that his is a history 'of madness' in the sense of a subjective, not an objective genitive; that, in other words, he is somehow writing from the standpoint of the mad themselves, not just showing how the mad have been perceived by the sane. In fact, the 600 pages between the preface and the conclusion deal almost exclusively with the latter perception. But we should not let this quantitative imbalance obscure the fact that 'madness in itself' is a central presence in this book.

Foucault insists on this presence because, at this stage, he is writing in opposition to the Enlightenment. Like Horkheimer and Adorno (in their *Dialectic of Enlightenment* some twenty years earlier), he has realized that the reason that was supposed to liberate us has itself become the primary instrument of our domination. The violent sarcasm of his rhetoric is a direct assault on the pretensions of reason, and his heroization of the mad aims to set up an alternative to the regime of reason. This alternative is the irrationally transgressive experience lived by the mad and evoked in the works of mad artists.

The problem with this move is the inadequacy of the 'experience' to which it appeals. As Foucault himself put it in a brief self-critique at the beginning of *The Archaeology of Knowledge*: 'Generally speaking, [*The History of Madness*] accorded far too great a place, and a very enigmatic one too, to what I called an "experience", thus showing to what extent one was still close to admitting an anonymous and general subject of experience' (AK, 16, translation modified). As I see it—without pretending to say this is just what Foucault had in mind—the inadequacy is at least threefold. First, there is the core truth of Kantianism: an experience, simply to be an experience, must have an object that it encounters as part of a world in which the object has a specific intelligibility. As a result, there is no coherent sense to an experience that is not informed by conceptual structures that define a space of reasons and hence norms of rationality. Second, the experience allegedly lived by the mad would be an ahistorical constant, passed on unchanged from period to period, unaffected by the forces that transform the human world. Foucault's strongly historical understanding has no place for such an autonomous experience. Finally, even if, contrary to the first two points, such an experience is possible, its radically amorphous, merely transgressive nature makes it entirely inadequate as a basis for the sort of specific political actions needed for effective opposition to systems of domination. Successful action requires a specific programme that cannot be grounded in the unstructured explosion of madness. A revolution requires controlled demolition-work, not random lightning flashes.

Foucault may have never entirely freed himself from his fascination with this arational experience. But he did eventually realize that it was not a meaningful alternative to Enlightenment reason. This shows up in his rejection of 'the blackmail of the Enlightenment' ('What Is Enlightenment?', EW III, 312), which he understands as the insistence that 'one has to be "for" or "against" the Enlightenment' (EW III, 313). Here he now sees that 'the Enlightenment' is 'a set of political, economic, social, institutional, and cultural events on which we still depend in large part' and that, as a result, 'constitutes a privileged domain for analysis' (EW III, 312). Viewed this way, the Enlightenment is like the air we breathe—an integral part of our existence that is too close to be an object of our choice, for or against. We can and must, instead, engage with it through 'a series of historical inquiries that are as precise as possible' (EW III, 313). Reason is part of what we are, although a part that requires constant analysis and adjustment. But there is no sense to the global challenge to reason that Foucault envisaged in his *History of Madness*.

The romance of a 'voice' of the mad can still have a role in our grappling with reason, but only as a generic reminder that we should never be entirely satisfied with our current deployment of reason. Just as the concept of truth serves as a caution that even claims we have 'justified to the hilt' might turn out to be false, so the idea of madness serves as a caution that what we currently regard as rational may someday turn out to be irrational. But for the later Foucault this entirely general caution has no specific significance in our wrestling with the reason that the Enlightenment has made part of our historical fate.

In the essay on Canguilhem mentioned in Chapter 6, Foucault developed a new concept that provides the specificity that the experience of the mad lacks. This is the notion of 'error', understood as a particular deviation from the norms of our epistemic environment. Although errors have typically been regarded as simply negative—as failures to reach the truth—Foucault notes that this is so only relative to a particular conceptualization of reality. From a broader perspective, what is an error in one framework of knowledge may turn out to be the seminal truth in developing a new framework of knowledge. For example, Copernicus' thought that the Earth moves around the Sun is an error in the purely negative sense in the world of Aristotelian and Ptolemaic astronomy. But it becomes the basis for the new astronomy of the 17th century. In this way, knowledge must itself be understood as a form of error.

This idea of knowledge-as-error is a specific and effective counterpart to Foucault's earlier embrace of the transgressive experiences of the mad (and, more generally, of avant-garde art). Error is itself a kind of transgression, a violation of the boundaries set by our conceptual environment. It is a localized and mundane version of the cosmic lightning flashes of madness. But what error lacks in metaphysical drama is more than compensated by its historical effectiveness. Precisely because it represents a specific deviation from particular norms, rather than an unfocused revolt against the very idea of normativity, error effects a practical change of the world we live in, not an aesthetic escape from it. In the end, Foucault subordinates the ecstasy of madness to the ironic satisfaction of (creative) error.

Foucault

Chapter 8
Crime and punishment

On 5 January 1757, Robert Damiens, 42 years old and a former soldier in the French army, rushed up to Louis XV with a knife and inflicted a light wound. He surrendered without a struggle and claimed that he had only intended to frighten, not kill, the king. Nonetheless, he was found guilty of regicide (indeed, parricide, since the king was the father of his people) and executed less than two months later. The execution was public, with a large crowd attending, and spectacularly brutal. Foucault opens *Discipline and Punish* with excruciating details, taken from eyewitness accounts, of how Damiens was drawn and quartered. Without stopping to comment on the horrifying text, he abruptly switches to another document, from 1837, just eighty years later, which states the rules for a detention centre for young offenders in Paris: 'The prisoner's day will begin at six in the morning in winter and five in the summer. They will work for nine hours a day throughout the year. Two hours a day will be devoted to instruction. Work and the day will end at nine o'clock in winter and at eight in the summer' (cited in DP, 6). After citing this and eleven similar rules, Foucault finally ventures a comment: 'We have, then, a public execution and a time-table' (DP, 7).

Two exemplary modes of punishment: the first occurred late enough in the Enlightenment to attract considerable criticism, but it typified the punishment of criminals in Europe until about the middle of the 18th century; the second represented the new, 'gentler' way of punishment, the product, it would seem, of a more civilized, more humane approach to punishment. On Foucault's account, this second stage eventually led to the full-blown modern system of what he calls 'discipline'.

Is the new idea—roughly, to imprison rather than to torture—the enlightened, progressive development it thinks it is? Foucault has his doubts, suggesting that the point was 'not to punish less, but to punish better' (DP, 82).

He begins by outlining the contrasts between modern and premodern approaches. There are four major transitions:

(1) Punishment is no longer a public display, a spectacular demonstration to all of the sovereign's irresistible *force majeure*, but rather a discreet, almost embarrassed application of constraints needed to preserve public order.

(2) What is punished is no longer the crime but the criminal, the concern of the law being not so much what criminals have done as what (environment, heredity, parental actions) has led them to do it.

(3) Those who determine the precise nature and duration of the punishment are no longer the judges who impose penalties in conformity with the law, but the 'experts' (psychiatrists, social workers, parole boards) who decide how to implement indeterminate judicial sentences.

(4) The avowed purpose of punishment is no longer retribution (either to deter others or for the sake of pure justice) but the reform and rehabilitation of the criminal.

Foucault does not deny that no longer ripping criminals apart is an advance. But the darker converse of the 'gentler' way is its penchant for total control. On one level, this is signalled by a switch from brutal, but unfocused, physical punishment to less painful but more intrusive psychological control. Premodern punishment violently assaults the criminal body, but is satisfied with retribution through pain; modern punishment demands an inner transformation, a conversion of the heart to a new way of life. But this modern control of the soul is itself a means to a more subtle and pervasive control of the body, since the point of changing psychological attitudes and tendencies is to control bodily behaviour. As Foucault puts it, for the modern age, 'the soul is the prison of the body' (DP, 30).

The most striking thesis of *Discipline and Punish* is that the disciplinary techniques introduced for criminals become the model for other modern sites of control (schools, hospitals, factories, etc.), so that prison discipline pervades all of modern society. We live, Foucault says, in a 'carceral archipelago' (DP, 298).

So, for example, the distinctive features of modern disciplinary control are apparent in the new approach to military training, the training designed to make ordinary people willing and able to kill the enemy. Premodern training centred on finding good material to begin with: men who had strength, good bearing, natural courage, etc., and then motivating them in a general way through pride and fear. But modern soldiers are produced through intense and specialized training, even if they are not initially especially fit. Boot camp 'makes' you a soldier. It's not a matter of the natural attractiveness of a model or an actor; the point is not to look like a soldier but to actually be a soldier—something that requires systematic training.

Disciplinary training is distinctive first because it operates not by direct control of the body as a whole but by detailed control of specific parts of the body. To teach soldiers to care for and shoot a rifle, we break the process down into an ordered succession of precise steps. It's not just a matter of showing them the entire operation and saying 'Do it like this.' The focus is not merely on the results to be achieved, of seeing that, one way or another, the soldier does what we desire. The point is rather to achieve the results through a specific set of procedures. We don't just want you to shoot the gun at the enemy; we want you to hold it just this way, raise it to your shoulder this way, sight down the barrel this way, pull the trigger this way. In short, it's a matter of micro-management. Foucault sums up the modern approach to discipline by saying that it aims at producing 'docile bodies': bodies that not only do what we want but do it precisely in the way that we want (DP, 138).

Docile bodies are produced through three distinctively modern means. *Hierarchical observation* is based on the obvious fact that we can control what people do merely by observing them. The watchtowers along city walls are a classic example. But modern power has raised the technique to a new level. Previously, architecture was an expression of the privileged status of those in power, either to display their magnificence ('the ostentation of palaces') or to give them a vantage point to overlook their subjects or enemies ('the geometry of fortresses') (DP, 172). But modern architecture builds structures that fulfil the functional needs of ordinary people and at the same time 'render visible those who are inside'. So, for example, the tiered rows of seats in a lecture hall, or well-lit classrooms with large windows and wide aisles, not only facilitate learning; they also make it extremely easy for teachers to see what everyone is doing. Similar techniques are at work in hospital rooms, military barracks, and factory work floors, all examples of 'an architecture that would operate to transform individuals: to act on those it shelters, to provide a hold on their conduct...to make it possible to know them, to alter them' (DP, 172).

For Foucault, the ideal architectural form of modern disciplinary power is Jeremy Bentham's Panopticon, a proposal for maximizing control of prisoners with a minimal staff (Figure 9). Although prisons approximating the Panopticon were not built until the 20th century, its principle has come to pervade modern society. In the Panopticon each inmate is in a separate cell, separated from and invisible to all the others. Further, the cells are distributed in a circle around a central tower from which a monitor can look into any cell at any given time. The principle of control is not the fact but the possibility of observation. The monitor will actually look into a given cell only occasionally. But the inmates have no way of knowing when these occasions will arise and so must always assume that they are being observed. The result is that we 'induce in the inmate a state of consciousness and permanent visibility that assures the automatic functioning of power' (DP, 201).

A second distinctive feature of modern disciplinary control is its concern with *normalizing judgement*. Individuals are judged not by the intrinsic rightness or wrongness of their acts but by where their actions place them on a ranked scale that compares them to everyone else. Children must not simply learn to read but must be in the 50th percentile of their reading group. A restaurant must not merely provide good food but be one of the top ten establishments in the city. This idea of normalization is pervasive in our society. On the official level, we set national standards for educational programmes, for medical practice, for industrial processes and products; less formally, we have an obsession with lists that rank-order everything from tourist sites, to our body weights, to levels of sexual activity.

Normalizing judgement (Figure 10) is a peculiarly pervasive means of control. There is no escaping it because, for virtually any level of achievement, the scale shows that there is an even higher level possible. Further, norms define certain modes of behaviour as 'abnormal', which puts them beyond the pale of what is socially (or even humanly) acceptable, even if they are far from the blatant transgressions that called for the excessive violence of premodern power. The threat of being judged abnormal constrains us moderns at every turn.

Finally, the *examination* combines hierarchical observation with normative judgement. It is, Foucault says, 'a normalizing gaze

9. Panoptic prison design, Illinois State Penitentiary, 1954.

[that] establishes over individuals a visibility through which one differentiates them and judges them'. The examination is a prime locus of modern power/knowledge, since it combines into a unified whole 'the deployment of force and the establishment of truth' (DP, 184). It both elicits the truth about those (patients, students, job candidates) who undergo the examination and, through the norms it sets, controls their behaviour.

10. Foucault and the judges, during the filming of *Moi, Pierre Riviere*.

The examination also reveals the new position of the individual in the modern nexus of power/knowledge. It situates individuals in a 'network of writing' (DP, 189). The results of examinations are recorded in documents that provide detailed information about the individuals examined and allow power systems to control them (for example, absentee records for schools, patients' charts in hospitals). On the basis of these records, those in control can formulate categories, averages, and norms that are in turn a basis for knowledge. The examination turns the individual into a 'case'—in both senses of the term: a scientific example and an object of care (and, of course, for Foucault, caring implies controlling). This process also reverses the polarity of visibility. In the premodern period, the exercise of power was itself typically highly visible (military presence in towns, public executions), while those who were the objects of knowledge remained obscure. But in the modern age the exercise of power is typically invisible, but it controls its objects by making them highly visible. And the highest visibility now belongs to those (criminals, the mad) whose thick dossiers are maintained and scrutinized by armies of anonymous and invisible functionaries.

83

On one level, *Discipline and Punish* does for prisoners what *The History of Madness* did for the mad. It analyses our allegedly humanitarian treatment of a marginalized group and shows how that treatment involves its own form of domination. In contrast to the book on madness, the analysis focuses more on the causal origins of institutional structures and less on systems of thought; it is, that is to say, more genealogical than archaeological. But this is a difference in emphasis only, since, as we have seen, the genealogy of *Discipline and Punish* is based on an archaeology of thought about the prison, and *The History of Madness* has a central concern with the institutional consequences of our perceptions of madness.

What most sets *Discipline and Punish* apart from its predecessor is the idea that the prison-model has metastasized throughout modern society. As a result, the book is not, like *The History of Madness*, centred on a specific Other against which 'we' (normal society) define ourselves. Society itself appears as a multitude of dominated others: not only criminals but also students, patients, factory workers, soldiers, shoppers. Each of us is—and in a variety of ways—the subject of modern power. Correspondingly, there is no single centre of power, no privileged 'us' against which a marginalized 'them' is defined. Power is dispersed throughout society, in a multitude of micro-centres. This dispersion corresponds to the fact that there is no teleology (no dominating class or world-historical process) behind the development. Modern power is the chance outcome, in the manner of genealogy, of numerous small, uncoordinated causes.

Foucault's picture of modern power challenges the premises of most revolutionary movements, in particular, Marxism. These movements identify specific groups and institutions (for example, the bourgeoisie, the central bank, the military high command, the government press) as sources of domination, the destruction or appropriation of which will lead to liberation. In the premodern world, when power was effectively centralized in the royal court and a few related institutions, such a revolution could be successful. The Marxists are like military strategists who plan to fight the previous war; taking the French Revolution as their model, they are trying to cut off the head of the king in a world where there is no king. Even after the government offices, the military bases, and the official newspapers are taken over, there remain countless other centres of power that resist the revolution. Foucault himself cited the Soviet Union as an 'example of a State apparatus which has changed hands, yet leaves social hierarchies, family life, sexuality and the body more or less as they were in capitalist society' (P/K, 'Questions on Geography', 73). The fundamental transformation the revolutionaries seek requires central control down to finest details of a nation's life. Here, perhaps, we have a Foucaultian explanation of the totalitarian thrust of modern revolutions.

This analysis suggests the reactionary conclusion that meaningful revolution, hence genuine liberation, is impossible: the only alternative to the modern net of micro-centres of power is totalitarian domination. Foucault would, I think, agree that these are the only global alternatives. But his conclusion would not be reactionary despair but a denial of the assumption that revolutionary liberation requires global transformation. For Foucault, politics—even revolutionary politics—is always local.

But locality itself is frequently a refuge of reaction. Particularly given Foucault's democratization of oppression—depending on the local context, we are all victims—how can he avoid dissipating effective revolution in an endless series of trivial protests? The bankers, the lawyers, the full professors will all have complaints of exploitation (as, for example, employees or consumers) that would seem to be as legitimate as any others. Here, however, Foucault can appeal to his notion of the *marginal,* his replacement, from the 1970s on, for the romantic idea of the mad as the radically Other. Marginalized individuals and groups are, unlike the mad, genuinely part of modern society; they speak its language (even if with an accent), share many of its values, play essential social and economic roles. At the same time, they are, in contrast to most of us, perpetually on the borders of society. This is for either or both of two reasons: their lives may be significantly defined by values that are counter to those of the social mainstream (think of homosexuals, members of non-standard religions, immigrants from non-Western cultures) or they may belong to a group whose welfare is systematically subordinated to that of mainstream groups (think of migrant workers, children in ghetto schools, street-walking prostitutes, inmates of penitentiaries).

In contrast to the mad, the marginalized have values that can meaningfully challenge our own and needs that could be plausibly satisfied within our society. Their concerns can, therefore, be the focus of programmes for effective political action. Further, such programmes can be genuinely revolutionary without Utopian global ambitions. For us to authentically say 'we' with the mad would require demolishing our core values and institutions, but the claims of the marginal are based on critiques of specific features of our society that can be modified without total overthrow.

It might seem that a politics of the marginal is itself just another instrument of marginalization, since it consists of 'our' claiming the right to speak for 'them'. Foucault was well aware of this danger and insisted on political actions designed simply to provide opportunities for marginalized groups to speak and be heard. So, for example, the Groupe d'Information sur les Prisons (GIP), which he, along with his companion, Daniel Defert, founded in the early 1970s, used Foucault's status as an intellectual celebrity to attract media attention to prisoners who spoke directly on their own behalf.

Marginality is the political counterpart of what we encountered earlier, in an epistemological context, as error. Politically, of course, error must be understood not only as the falsity of a proposition but also, non-linguistically, as inappropriate behaviour or misguided values. Foucaultian politics, as I am understanding it, is the effort to allow the 'errors' that marginalize a group to interact creatively with the 'truths' of the mainstream society. To the extent that the effort succeeds, the marginal group will no longer be a specific object of domination, and society as a whole will be transformed and enriched by what it had previously rejected as errors.

It may seem that what I am calling 'creative interaction' is just a cover for assimilating marginal groups into the social mainstream, and so destroying their most distinctive values. But interaction need not involve a levelling assimilation, particularly if it is achieved by giving the marginal group a serious voice in the terms of the interaction. On the other hand, there is the converse question of whether, or to what extent, a given marginal group is worth interacting with. We may, quite legitimately, decide that the needs and values of certain marginal groups (for example, neo-Nazis or apocalyptic religious cults) are simply incompatible with our basic values and that we can, at most, tolerate them.

A final difficulty: why should our political practice be so focused on marginal groups? Why not, for example, a neo-conservative politics of deepening our commitment to mainstream values or extending them to other societies? This is a crucial question for those who, like Foucault, share the liberal assumption that self-critique and appreciation of the Other should be at the heart of our political agenda. Unfortunately, unlike liberals such as John Rawls, Foucault has little to offer in response. His own political stance seems to derive simply from his own individual commitment to constant self-transformation. His focus on marginal groups follows from his horror of being stuck in an identity. Here, for Foucault, the political is at root personal. To those who do not share his horror, he can only reply—in words he once deployed in a similar context—'We are not from the same planet' (UP, 7).

Chapter 9
Modern sex

Because he was homosexual, writing a history of modern sexuality must have been a particularly personal enterprise for Foucault. His biographers suggest that as an adolescent he suffered from having sexual interests that French society of the 1940s and 1950s regarded mostly with shame or outrage. Even the generally tolerant milieu of the École Normale was not entirely hospitable to homosexuality. Foucault makes it clear that one of his reasons for accepting a job in Sweden was the hope, not entirely fulfilled, of finding a more open sexual climate. Even though the details of Foucault's sex life remain sketchy—and why shouldn't they?—there is every reason to think that the experience of gay marginality was an important part of his life. On the other hand, he was as unwilling to accept the identity of 'homosexual' as he was any other. He seldom wrote or spoke on record as a 'gay man', and, when he did—for example, in a few interviews with gay publications—his attitude toward the activist gay community is more that of a sympathetic observer than a committed participant. He is most attracted by what he sees as recent gay explorations of new forms of human community and identity.

In any case, homosexuality was just one of many topics to be covered by Foucault's history of sexuality, which in addition to a volume called 'Perverts' would also have volumes on children, women, and married couples. Moreover, his general introduction to the project, the only volume of the series actually published, shows that, as in *Discipline and Punish*, his treatment would expand beyond marginalized groups to everyone in modern society. In fact, it seems clear that, from the beginning, Foucault's work on sexuality was developing a dimension beyond that of power relations. It was becoming a history of the formation of subjects in not only a political but also a psychological and ethical sense.

The starting point is, however, still Foucault's conception of modern power, which is most explicitly set out in Volume I of the *History of Sexuality*. As a result, Foucault's initial treatment of sexuality is a fairly straightforward extension of the genealogical method of *Discipline and Punish*. The method is applied to the various modern bodies of knowledge about sexuality ('sciences of sexuality') in order to show their intimate association with the power structures of modern society. The focus of this aspect of Foucault's discussion is what he calls the 'repressive hypothesis'. This is the common assumption that the primary attitude of modern society toward sex (beginning in the 18th century, reaching a peak in the Victorian age, and still exerting strong influence today) was negative; that, except for the closely delimited sphere of monogamous marriage, sexuality was opposed, silenced, and, as far as possible, eliminated.

Foucault does not deny the fact of repression. The Victorian age covered bosoms, censored literature, and waged vigorous campaigns against masturbation. But he denies that modern power is primarily exercised through repression and that opposition to repression is an effective way of resisting modern power. Rather, he thinks that modern power created new forms of sexuality by inventing discourses about it. For example, although same-sex relations have occurred throughout human history, the homosexual as a distinct category, with defining psychological, physiological, and perhaps even genetic characteristics, was created by the power/knowledge system of the modern sciences of sexuality.

According to Foucault, sexual repression is a superficial phenomenon; far more significant is the 'veritable discursive explosion' (HS, 17) of talk about sex that began in the 17th century, with the Counter-Reformation's legislation on the practice of confession. Penitents were required to 'examine their consciences' with a thoroughness and nuance previously unheard of. It was not enough to say 'I slept with a woman other than my wife'; you had to say how many times, just what sorts of acts were involved, whether the woman was herself married. Nor was it enough to report overt actions. Equally important were thoughts and desires, even if not carried out. But even here it was not enough to say, 'I thought about sleeping with a woman other than my wife'. You also had to determine if you had dwelt on the thought, found enjoyment in it rather than rejecting it immediately; and, if you had entertained it, whether this was done with a certain inadvertence or with 'full consent of the will'. All these factors were needed for the confessor to determine the degree of guilt (for example, mortal versus venial sin), impose an appropriate penance, and give advice for moral improvement. The result for penitents was an ever deeper and more precise self-knowledge, the outcome of a 'hermeneutics of the self' that revealed as fully as possible their inner sexual natures. Foucault's suggestion, however, is that this nature is not so much discovered as constituted by the required self-examination. What I am sexually depends on the categories I am required to use in making my confession.

A large part of the history of modern sexuality is the secular adaptation and expansion of these religious techniques of self-knowledge. Confession may no longer be made to a priest but it is surely made to one's doctor, psychiatrist, best friend, or, at least, to oneself. And the categories that define the possibilities of one's sexual nature are not self-chosen but accepted on the authority of 'experts' in the new modern sciences of sexuality: the Freuds, the Krafft-Ebings, the Havelock Ellises, the Margaret Meads. Such experts present as discoveries about human nature what are actually just new social norms for behaviour.

Of course, there is a distinction between sexuality as a social construct and sex as a biological reality. Foucault does not deny that there are, for example, undeniable physiological facts about human reproduction. But he maintains that once we move from sheer biology to the inevitably hermeneutic and normative concepts of psychology, anthropology, etc., the distinction breaks down. The Oedipal complex, for example, is tied to assumptions about the meaning and value of the bourgeois family; it is not just another fact, like the physiology of conception. Even what seem to be simple biological facts, for example, the distinction of male and female, can turn out to have normative social significance, as is demonstrated by the case of Herculine Barbin, a 19th-century hermaphrodite, who was raised as a female but, in her twenties, came under the scrutiny of doctors who decided that she was in fact a man and forced her to live as one. Foucault published the poignant memoirs Barbin wrote before committing suicide at the age of 30.

Given his critique of the repressive hypothesis, Foucault is able to develop a history of sexuality that often parallels his history of the prison. Just as the modern sciences of criminology define categories of social dysfunction (juvenile delinquent, kleptomaniac, drug addict, serial killer, etc.) that are simultaneously sources of knowledge and of control regarding their 'subjects', so the modern sciences of sexuality define categories of sexual dysfunction (homosexual, nymphomaniac, fetishist, etc.) that have a parallel role as power/knowledge.

Foucault cites as an example the case of Charles Jouy, a 40-year-old farm worker, who lived in rural France in the 1860s. Jouy, illegitimate and uneducated, lived at the margins of his village's society, the 'village idiot', paid at the lowest level for work no one else would do. Women and older girls mocked him when he showed sexual interest. But a young girl, Sophie Adam, agreed to play with him a game of masturbation that was common among young boys and girls of the area. Shortly afterward, during a village fair, Jouy pulled Adam into a ditch (or, Foucault suggests, perhaps Adam pulled him). After what Foucault says was 'almost rape, perhaps', Jouy gave her a small payment and she ran off to buy some almonds. Foucault describes this activity as 'harmless embraces', but Adam's mother found out what had happened and reported Jouy to the authorities, who brought down upon him the full brunt of the new science of sexuality. Prominent outside experts carried out detailed legal and medical examinations. Jouy was found guilty of no crimes but was diagnosed as an 'imbecile', with corresponding bodily degeneracy, and confined to an asylum for the rest of his life as a 'pure object of medicine and knowledge' (HS, 32). The villagers decided that Sophie Adam should be sent to a 'house of correction' to overcome her 'bad tendencies' (*Abnormal*, 295).

Foucault's response to this case has raised many eyebrows:

> What is the significant thing about this story? The pettiness of it all; the fact that this everyday occurrence in the life of village sexuality, these inconsequential bucolic pleasures, could become, from a certain time, the object not only of a collective intolerance but of a judicial action, a medical intervention, a careful clinical examination, and an entire theoretical elaboration.

> (HS, 31)

His remarks particularly disturb feminists, who have long fought against male trivialization of the sexual mistreatment of women. Linda Alcoff made an influential case against Foucault's 'masculinist' assumption that Jouy was the victim, with no thought that he had sexually molested a child, with very likely traumatic effects. With 'typical male and adult patterns of epistemic arrogance', she says, Foucault shows no interest in what happened to Sophie Adam and lends support to the long discredited excuse that children are often willing sexual partners of adults. Although most feminists basically agree with

Alcoff, Shelley Tremain has offered a spirited critique, arguing that Alcoff mistakenly assumes that modern medical/legal categories make sense in Jouy's distinctly premodern world. She also tries to turn the tables on Alcoff, suggesting that, in today's terms, Jouy suffers from a disability that requires empathetic assistance, not moral condemnation.

Foucault envisaged four further volumes on modern sexuality. Three of these were to treat specific marginalized groups: children, as the object of the campaign to suppress masturbation (*The Children's Crusade*); women as subjects of the sexually based disorder of hysteria (*The Hysterical Woman*); and homosexuals and other groups judged sexually 'abnormal' (*Perverts*). All these groups, like the criminals of *Discipline and Punish*, were constituted and controlled by hierarchical observation and normalizing judgements. Further, as in the case of criminality, there was no real possibility of eliminating or even substantially reducing the targeted behaviours, so the de facto function of the power apparatus was simply to control segments of the population. A fourth projected volume was *The Malthusian Couple*, where Foucault's topic would have been various power structures designed to limit the population and improve its quality. This, again as in *Discipline and Punish*, is readily seen as an extension of disciplinary power to non-marginal groups.

In the concluding chapter of the introduction to *The History of Sexuality*, Foucault seems to be moving beyond sexuality as such and develops a notion of bio-power, which embraces all the forms of modern power directed toward us as living beings, that is, as subject to standards of not just sexual but biological normality. Bio-power is concerned with the 'task of administering life', a process that operates on two levels. On the level of individuals, there is an 'anatomo-politics of the human body'; on the level of social groups, there is a 'bio-politics of populations' (HS, 139. The first level implicitly complements the primarily epistemological treatment of medicine in *The Birth of the Clinic*, making explicit the political significance (in a broad sense that includes the social and the economic) of the medical norms defining a healthy individual. So, for example, the modern medical notion of obesity corresponds to the marginalized social class of 'fat people', and modern techniques of drug treatments of illness are inextricably tied to the economics of the pharmaceutical industry. The second level concerns the modern focus on a nation's entire population as a resource that must be protected, supervised, and improved. Thus, capitalism requires universal medical care and education to ensure an adequate workforce; racist ideologies call for eugenic measures to protect the purity of the population 'stock'; and military planners develop the concept of 'total war', as a battle between not just armies but entire populations. We see, then, that Foucault's project of a history of modern sexuality was, even as he began it, expanding to a history of modern bio-power.

Perhaps even more significant was another direction of expansion, toward what Foucault came to call a 'history of the subject'. This had already begun to emerge in *Discipline and Punish*, where Foucault (Figure 11) occasionally noted how the objects of disciplinary control could themselves internalize the norms whereby they were controlled and so become monitors of their own behaviour. In the context of sexuality, this phenomenon becomes central, since individuals are supposed to discern their own fundamental nature as sexual beings and, on the basis of this self-knowledge, transform their lives. As a result, we are controlled not only as *objects* of disciplines that have expert knowledge of us; we are also controlled as self-scrutinizing and self-forming *subjects* of our own knowledge. This new perspective leads Foucault to question the modern ideal of sexual liberation. I discover my deep sexual nature through self-scrutiny and come to express this nature by overcoming various hang-ups and neuroses. But am I really freeing myself, or am I just reshaping my life in accord with a new set of norms? Isn't promiscuity as demanding an ideal as monogamy, the imperative to be sexually adventurous as

11. Foucault in 1979.

burdensome as a prudish limitation to the missionary position? The magazines, self-help books, and sex manuals that guide us to a life of liberated sexuality seem to induce in us as much insecurity and fear about our sexual attractiveness and ability to perform as sermons and tracts did in our grandparents about the dangers of sexual indulgence. More importantly, is my acceptance of the demands of liberation any more an expression of my 'true nature' than were our grandparents' acceptance of the demands of traditional morality? Foucault suggests that, in both cases, the acceptance may merely be an internalization of external norms. The irony of our endless preoccupation with our sexuality, Foucault says, is that we think that it has something to do with liberation (HS, 159).

Foucault's new perspective led him to the view that his study of sexuality was really part of an effort to understand the process whereby individuals become subjects. He was, he concluded, writing not so much a history of sexuality as a history of the subject. This transition arose from the fact that he had found sexuality to be an integral part of our identity as selves or subjects. To say that I am homosexual or that I am obsessed with Albertine is to say something central about what I am in the concreteness of my subjectivity. Here Foucault seems to return to the standpoint of individual consciousness, which he earlier rejected in his choice of the philosophy of the concept over the philosophy of experience. I, however, would suggest that he never really left this standpoint, but instead rejected transcendental readings of subjectivity that ignored its fundamentally historical nature. In any case, he now felt the ability and the need to give an account of the historical process whereby we become subjects. The question is not how consciousness emerges from unconscious matter but how a conscious being assumes a particular identity, that is, comes to think of itself as directed by a given set of ethical norms, which give its existence a specific meaning and purpose.

In *The History of Sexuality*, Foucault began looking at the way the modern consciousness of an ethical self emerged through the secularization of Christianity's hermeneutics of the self (as in the confessional practices we discussed above). His original plan was to develop this theme at length in a separate volume on medieval Christian views of sexuality. This was to be the second volume of the history of sexuality, followed by the four volumes, on children, women, perverts, and couples. (As we'll see in Chapter 11, Foucault did write a version of this volume, but didn't live to publish it.)

But as Foucault reflected further on his project, he decided that he needed to begin not with the Middle Ages but with ancient Greek and Roman views on sexuality and the self. He had concluded that to properly understand the Christian hermeneutic view of the self, he had to trace its origins and differences from ancient ideas. He began brushing up his schoolboy Greek and Latin and had many discussions with two of his friends and colleagues in the Collège de France: Paul Veyne, a Roman historian, and Pierre Hadot, a historian of ancient philosophy. This major redirection, combined with ill health (which turned out to be the AIDS from which Foucault eventually died), seriously delayed the project. It was only in 1984, just before his death, that Foucault was able to publish two volumes on the ancient world: *The Use of Pleasure*, which discussed Greek texts of the 4th century BC, and *The Care of the Self*, which covered Greek and Roman texts from the 1st century BC to the 1st century AD.

Although these books were titled Volume II and Volume III of Foucault's *History of Sexuality*, there is no sense in which Volume I, which we have been discussing here, can be regarded as an introduction to them. Put roughly, the project Volume I is introducing is one in which modern sexuality would be studied as an example of bio-power: biological (in a broad sense) knowledge as a basis for socio-political control of individuals and groups. This is a project Foucault never carried out, although there are some elements of it dispersed in his writings before and after Volume I. Volumes II and III are part of a study of ancient sexuality as an example of the ethical formation of the self. There is no overlap with the earlier interest in bio-power, although there is a connection through the shared topic of the Christian hermeneutics of the self. It was misleading for Foucault to present these two books as continuations of his original history of sexuality. He may have envisaged some broader project that would have approached sexuality through both bio-power and the formation of the self. But at the end of his life he seems to have rather been moving away from the history of sexuality. His new direction, as we shall see, connects the formation of the subject not to sexuality but to what he came to call 'games of truth'.

Chapter 10
Ancient sex

Those who have struggled with the obscurities of Foucault's archly intense prose are vastly relieved by the easy lucidity with which he writes in his last two books. Had his final illness led to a peaceful reconciliation reflected in his writing? Or was it merely that, wanting to finish this project before he died, he didn't have time for baroque complexification? Rather, I think, Foucault had entered a world that was removed from the present he so often found 'intolerable' and that suggested modes of existence he found immensely appealing.

His topic, the ethical formation of the self, emerged, of course, from his analysis of modern power relations, which he saw penetrating even the interiority of our personal identity. No doubt the reason he so resisted any fixed identity was his realization that even what might seem to be his own autonomous choice of identity could be just an internalization of social norms. But, as Foucault traces the historical constitution of ethical identity back beyond the Christian hermeneutics of the self and its modern secular successors, dominating power comes to have little place in his story.

He still plays on the duality of the term 'subject', speaking now of the 'modes of subjectification', whereby an ethical code enters individuals' lives and constitutes their identity. And his general structure of subjectification—derived from an archaeological analysis of ancient texts—is certainly open to power relations. This structure involves, as its basis, the acts that concern sexual behaviour (what the Greeks called *ta aphrodisia*—the 'things of Aphrodite' and what Foucault labels the 'ethical substance'). It further involves the sense in which individuals are made subject to the ethical code. This, which Foucault calls the 'mode of subjection', might be a matter of anything from conforming to social conventions to carrying out a programme of self-fulfilment. Beyond the question of what it means to be subjected to the moral code is the question of the specific means by which the subjection is carried out, the 'forms of elaboration', which might, for example, include self-conscious following of practical rules or, on the contrary, a sudden, overwhelming conversion. Finally, there is the ultimate goal (*telos*) envisaged for the project of morality; for example, the attainment of self-mastery or purification for an afterlife.

Although this schema allows for the operation of power, the way Foucault applies it to ancient sexual ethics emphasizes ethical subjectification as something carried out by individuals who seem in control of their destiny. They might, to combine some of the above examples, be carrying out a project of self-fulfilment by meticulously following a set of practices ('techniques of the self') designed to produce self-mastery. Likewise, Foucault speaks, with apparent admiration, of the Greeks' 'aesthetics of existence', in which a life is created like a work of art. It also becomes apparent that Foucault's focus is much more general than sexual ethics. As he commented in an interview while working on *The Care of the Self*, 'I am much more interested in problems about techniques of the self…than sex—sex is boring' ('On the Genealogy of Ethics', EW I, 253).

But, we will point out, Foucault himself has already shown, especially in the *History of Sexuality I*, that there can be only an illusion of self-creation. What we may think is our freedom is, like modern sexual liberation, only an internalization of the constraints of power relations. Foucault may be attracted by the ancients' project of creating beautiful lives, but he of all people is surely aware that this very project is entwined with the power structures of Greek society. Consider, for example, the Greek practice of homosexual love between men and adolescent boys. Even though this is free of Christian strictures about intrinsically evil, unnatural acts, it is, as Foucault emphasizes in *The Use of Pleasure*, problematized for political reasons. The boy, who is sought as the passive partner of a dominating male, is nonetheless being groomed as a future leader of the *polis*. How could such a person be a sexual object on the same level as women and slaves? For all of Plato's talk of ideal beauty and the soul's self-mastery, the issue of 'Platonic love' cannot be detached from the power relations of Athenian society.

The key to this issue is the concept of *problematization*, which I have just casually introduced but which is in fact a key notion of Foucault's later thought. Problematizations formulate the fundamental issues and choices through which individuals confront their existence. The fact that my existence is problematized in a specific way is no doubt determined by the social power relations in which I am embedded. But, given this problematization, I am able to respond to the issues it raises in my own way, or, more precisely, in a way by which I will define what I, as a self, am in my historical context.

There is an implied contrast—although Foucault never makes it explicit—between problematization and marginalization. In the ancient context where he introduces the term, it is the lives of free Greek males that are problematized, not those of marginalized groups such as women and slaves. Marginalization corresponds to the strongest constraints that a society exercises on individuals. Even the marginalized are not entirely determined by a society's power structures, since they are capable of engaging (and succeeding) in revolutionary movements against what dominates them. But they can define themselves only through their struggle with power. The 'mainstream' members of a society, those who are not marginalized, are less constrained. The power network defines them in a preliminary way but allows for a significant range of further self-definition. Unlike the marginalized, they have available 'niches' within the society that provide them room for self-formation in their own terms. The 'problematization' of the free Greek male lies in this domain.

My suggestion is that, in moving to the history of the subject (and to the history of ancient sexuality), Foucault implicitly switches his primary focus from those whose lives are marginalized to those whose lives are merely problematized. In this way, without denying the pervasiveness of power, he tacitly acknowledges that it allows some people to lead lives of relative freedom and self-creation. In ancient Greece, this included at least some free males; in our world it includes, among others, those of us who have the ability and opportunity to write and read books like Foucault's.

It may seem that problematization is a third Foucaultian historical method, supplementing (or replacing) archaeology and genealogy. Strictly speaking, this is false, since problematization is not a historical method but an object studied by such methods. The turn to problematization is a switch from marginalized to problematized individuals. But Foucault's way of engaging with ancient problematizations of sexuality does involve a major change in his historical methodology. He first requires a careful exploration of the structures of ancient discourses about sexuality, for which archaeology is, of course, the primary instrument. At the same time, he has little concern with the power relations that are entwined with ancient knowledge of sexuality. *The Use of Pleasure* refers, as we have noted, to the political roots of the 'problem of the boy', and *The Care of the Self* has a brief (and, by Foucault's own admission, quite derivative) chapter on the social forces behind the transition from Greek to Roman views of sexuality.

But the genealogy of power, in the sense of Foucault's earlier work, is muted in these two books.

This is because genealogy is concerned with the lines of power connected to our present system of domination. It is, as Foucault said in *Discipline and Punish*, a history of the present. But the power regimes of ancient Greece and Rome are too distant to figure in our understanding of our present power structures. When only these structures were Foucault's concern, he needed, as he originally planned, to go no further back than medieval notions of pastoral care. But once the topic became problematizations and self-creative responses to them—matters that develop in the interstices of a power regime—the ancients immediately became interesting. Not, however, because of the specific origin of their problems, which would require a genealogical study, but because of the kinds of creative responses the ancients gave to these problems.

Foucault is reluctant to give up the term 'genealogy', perhaps because it keeps him connected to Nietzsche. But he no longer presents genealogy as an instrument of suspicion, following the pervasive tracks of modern power. Instead, it is a (generally appreciative) account of the ancient world's 'arts of existence'; that is, of 'those intentional and voluntary actions by which men not only set themselves rules of conduct, but also seek to make their life an oeuvre that carries certain aesthetic values and meets certain stylistic criteria' (UP, 10–11). Beyond the word, there is little that remains here except the generic idea of a causal account of the self's formation. But this account is no longer a reconstruction of complex external lines of power but of internal programmes for ethical transformation. It is, in fact, much closer to history of philosophy than genealogy in Foucault's original sense. Or, perhaps better, it is philosophy itself done in a historical mode.

We will return to Foucault's final 'philosophy' below. But first we need to look at his archaeology of ancient sexuality, to understand how the Greeks and Romans problematized sexuality and what Foucault thought we might learn from their problematization. As always for Foucault, archaeology is a comparative matter. In this case, the fundamental comparison is with the Christian view of sexuality. Here he is once again Nietzschean, although without the rhetorical violence of *The Antichrist*: the rise of Christian sexuality is the corruption of a more admirable antique view. At the same time, Foucault makes it clear that there is no question of a return to the ways of the ancients, which have their own severe limitations and, in any case, could not exist in our world. Ancient ways can serve only as heuristic guides for own projects of self-creation.

According to Foucault, there are relatively few differences between the ancients and the Christians on the level of moral codes and conduct. The ethical rules laid down and the actual patterns of behaviour these rules determine are, despite some striking exceptions such as same-sex relations, quite similar. But fundamental differences arise when we look at the formation of ethical subjects.

The root of the differences, says Foucault, is the Christian claim that *ta aphrodisia* are intrinsically evil and so primarily objects of ethical denial. For the ancients, by contrast, sex was a natural good. It became an object of ethical problematization not because it was essentially forbidden but because some aspects of it could be dangerous. This was because the goods of sex were on the inferior level of our animality and because they often involved great intensity. The danger was not, as for the Christian, that they might become an important part of our lives—this the ancients saw as inevitable and fitting—but that we might disrupt our lives through excessive indulgence.

Accordingly, for the Christian, subjection to a code of sexual ethics was a matter of absolute exclusion, in the ideal of celibacy, or, at least, for the less heroic, restriction to the strictly limited domain of monogamous marriage. For the ancients, by contrast, it was a matter of the proper use (*chresis*) of pleasures; not avoiding certain essentially evil actions but engaging in the full range of sexual activities (heterosexual, homosexual, in marriage, out of marriage) with proper moderation (given, of course, the understanding that we are speaking of free males, not women and slaves).

In order to live according to their code of sexual behaviour, the ancients tried to attain self-mastery (*enkrateia*), victory in a struggle with oneself, achieved by the training (*askesis*) provided by exercises in self-control. For Christians, the battle was with outside forces of evil—ultimately Satan—that incite desires, and victory was through a radical understanding (hermeneutics) of the self that was the basis for a renunciation of this self in favour of God: not self-mastery but self-denial. Finally, the telos of ancient ethical life was moderation (*sophrysune*), understood as a form of freedom—both negative (from one's passions) and positive (as mastery over others). For Christianity, the only humanly meaningful freedom sought was the negative freedom from desires; beyond that there was merely total surrender to the will of God.

The sharp contrast with Christianity applies most to Classical Greek views of the 4th century BC. Later (early Empire) views of sexuality remain, according to Foucault, basically the same but with increasing emphases in the direction of Christian negativity. So, for example, although *ta aphrodisia* are still regarded as intrinsic goods, there is far more insistence on their dangers and on our frailty in face of them. Similarly, the techniques of self-mastery (*enkrateia*) remain central but are increasingly connected to self-knowledge, and into the ideal of *sophrysune* there is incorporated an element of contemplative satisfaction. Particularly through Stoic philosophy, the Roman world was planting seeds of the Christian revolution.

Foucault's account of Christian sexuality seems to ignore the central doctrine of the goodness of creation. Even Augustine, whom many see as a major source for the anti-sexual view Foucault outlines, insisted, against the Manichaeans, that there was nothing intrinsically evil in the world. Even the Fall, according to orthodox Catholic doctrine, did not radically corrupt any aspect of human nature, and all of creation, including our sexuality, is redeemed by Christ. Foucault might, of course, argue that these metaphysical and theological doctrines did not determine practical ethical teaching. But we would need to have his detailed account of medieval sexuality to know what he really thought. (We discuss the beginnings of this account in Chapter 11.)

I suggested earlier that at the end of his life what Foucault still called genealogy was becoming a kind of philosophy. I can best develop this thought by commenting on Foucault's final overall characterization of his work, in the Preface to *The Use of Pleasure*. He now maintains that, from the beginning, he has, on the broadest level, been developing a 'history of truth'. He conceives this history as having three main aspects: an analysis of 'games of truth' (that is, various systems of discourse developed to produce truth), both in their own right and in relation to one another; an analysis of the relation of these games of truth to power relations; and an analysis of the relation of games of truth to the self. We can readily identify the study of games of truth in their own right, as systems of discourse, with archaeology, and the analysis of their relation to power with genealogy. Here 'games of truth' refers to the various bodies of knowledge (real or would-be) that were the concern of Foucault's histories. It might seem natural to extend this sense of 'games of truth' to Foucault's connection of them with problematizations, taking as the relevant games the philosophical theories that the ancient Greeks developed as solutions to the problems of human existence.

However, although Foucault does indeed see philosophy as the Greek response to problematizations, he does not see philosophy in this sense as a matter of developing a body of theoretical knowledge. Rather, following on the work of Pierre Hadot, his colleague at the Collège de France, he sees ancient philosophy as fundamentally a way of life rather than a search for theoretical truth. 'Games of truth', in this context refers not to systems of thought but to practices of telling the truth. *The Use of Pleasure* discusses Plato's appeal to the love of truth as the purified ideal behind the homoerotic love of boys. Plato, however, has at least a strong tendency to treat philosophy as a theoretical vision rather than just a way of life, and Foucault is careful to keep his distance from this sort of Platonism.

The title of the last book Foucault published, *The Care of the Self*, refers to a major theme in the practically oriented philosophical schools of later antiquity, particularly the Stoics. But the book is mostly concerned with the theme in non-philosophical contexts, such as medicine, marriage, and politics. In Chapter 11 we will see how, in late, unpublished lectures, Foucault discussed philosophy as a way of life directed toward care of the self.

In any case, it seems that here, at the end of his life, Foucault had finally found a way to move beyond what, varying Paul Ricoeur's famous phrase, we might call the epistemology of suspicion. All his previous work had, as he claims, been about truth, but, in contrast to the traditional philosopher's unconditional love of truth, Foucault put truth to the test. His archaeologies show how it is often relative to the contingent historical frameworks it is supposed to transcend, his genealogies how it is entwined with the power and domination from which it is supposed to free us. Now he finds a way to embrace truth, not as a body of theoretical knowledge, but as a way of living: not an epistemology, but an ethics, of truth (Figure 12).

But what does Foucault mean by 'living the truth'? Not, of course, modelling ourselves on a pre-set ideal pattern, determined by, say, God's will or human nature. His study of the ancients, as we have

12. Foucault in a cowboy hat that his students at Berkeley gave him, October 1983.

seen, suggested two alternatives: truth as the product of individual self-creation on analogy with art; and truth-telling as a social virtue. Here, at the very end, we find again what may well be the defining dichotomy of Foucault's life and work: the aesthetic or the political?

Chapter 11
Foucault after Foucault

Foucault died far too young, leaving a large body of lectures and drafts unpublished (which, eighteen months before he died, he had instructed his heirs not to publish). Of particular importance were thirteen years of lectures he delivered at the Collège de France, where he held a chair from 1971 to 1984. (He had a sabbatical in 1977, so there were no lectures that year.) The Collège is a strictly research institution: there are no students enrolled or degrees awarded. Its professors are, however, required to 'teach' for twenty-six hours each year, dividing the time as they like between public lectures reporting on their current research and more specialized seminars discussing a specific topic with any interested scholars. Foucault fulfilled this obligation each January through March, typically splitting his hours evenly between lectures and seminars.

'No posthumous publications' was Foucault's injunction in a letter his heirs agreed to accept as his last will and testament. Like most such commands, from Vergil to Kafka, it was ineffective. If you want 'no posthumous publications', you need to destroy the manuscripts yourself. In Foucault's case, the heirs held the line for almost thirteen years. But in 1997 they made an exception for the Collège de France lectures, which Foucault had allowed attendees to tape, inevitably leading to the circulation of transcriptions. The heirs accepted the argument that Foucault's permission to tape was equivalent to permission to publish, so that books merely reproducing the transcriptions wouldn't be posthumous publications. Once this door was open, it was an easy step to refer to Foucault's own written versions of the lectures to supplement or correct the transcriptions (which themselves remained essential, since Foucault sometimes modified his written text and even improvised new material). But there were no tapes available for the first two courses, and the heirs allowed publication based on Foucault's drafts. By now a good number of other previously unpublished lectures, notes, interviews, etc. have appeared.

The lectures exhibit the twists and turns of a mind constantly processing new material and reformulating its ideas. Neither the series as a whole nor the individual sets of annual lectures present a fixed organizational structure. To the extent that Foucault reached conclusions, they appeared in the last four books he published (*Discipline and Punish* and the three volumes of the *History of Sexuality*). On Foucault's own self-deprecatory assessment, the lectures contain 'a lot of rubbish, but also lots of work and ways to take it that might be useful to the kids'. But we might also say that the lectures let us follow Foucault's circuitous process of discovery, a process that both illuminates his published work and provides stimulating hints of further possibilities.

The first year, *Lectures on the Will to Know*, did, among other things, set out a general theme that informs all thirteen years of lectures: the relation of truth and power (or, perhaps, the connection between epistemology and politics). The basic idea is nicely expressed in a passage from Georges Dumézil, *Servius et la Fortune*, that Foucault used as an epigraph for his 1981 lectures at Louvain on 'Wrong-Doing, Truth-Telling':

> As far back as we go in the behavior of our species, the 'true utterance' is a force to which few forces resist... Very early on, the Truth appeared to men as one of the most effective verbal weapons,

one of the most prolific seeds of power, one of the most solid foundations for their institutions.

The earlier lectures of this first series illustrate the historical scope of this idea, with discussions of truth and power in ancient authors (Hesiod, Sophocles, the Sophists, Plato, and Aristotle) as well as in Nietzsche. The later lectures turn to the modern period, which will be the focus of DP, which *Penal Theories and Institutions* (1971–2) and *The Punitive Society* (1972–3) anticipate. *Psychiatric Power* (1973–4) offers an important rethinking, not published elsewhere, of aspects of the *History of Madness* in light of Foucault's new ideas about power. *Abnormal* (1974–5) discusses various 'monsters' of crime and sexuality that appear in DP and HS. *Society Must Be Defended* (1975–6) develops Foucault's thinking on another major topic of these two books: war as the basis of society. Foucault retrospectively presented these first six lecture series as having a particular focus on normalization (roughly, power exercised through knowledge about what is 'normal').

In the next two lecture series, *Security, Territory, Population* (1977–8) and *The Birth of Biopolitics* (1978–9), Foucault introduces the notion of *government* into his thinking about power. Initially, the plan was just to analyse the political systems (governments) of contemporary liberal societies, to supplement his studies of disciplinary systems such as courts and prisons. This required making room for a highly structured centralized power hovering over the loose diversity of the micro-centres emphasized in his earlier studies. This focus on centralized government was a nod to mainstream political scientists, who had responded with considerable interest in Foucault's approach.

In analysing liberal governments, Foucault deployed two key concepts: *population*, a common term that he gives a special sense, and *governmentality*, a multi-syllabic abstraction that fits well with the jargon of political theorizing. Of course, all political units, from Palaeolithic tribes to the Roman Empire, have populations in the sense of the people its rulers control. Population in Foucault's sense is not only a political but also an epistemic category: a population is the object of modern bodies of medical, economic, and sociological knowledge, based on sophisticated statistical methods, that are instruments of its governance. Governmentality, then, is the ensemble of 'institutions, procedures, analyses, and reflections, the calculations and tactics that make possible the exercise of this power that has as its principal target the population' (*Security, Territory, Population*, 102).

Because liberal governments rely so heavily on the rational processes of gathering and analysing data, they can assert their authority not only through brute force or blind faith but also by offering the population plausible reasons for accepting governmental policies. Persuasion thus becomes a major instrument of power. But giving reasons opens the door to questioning the reasons, so that the population ceases to be a passive mass and assumes an active role in political life. Responding to critique becomes an essential governmental function. Of course, the models for such interactions range from ideals of respectful discourse to travesties of manipulative propaganda.

Characteristically, Foucault sought further understanding of contemporary governmentality by constructing a genealogy of its origins. He does not see it emerging from ancient Greek or Roman governance but from the pastoral care of the Christian Church (a practice that comes to interest Foucault more and more). Later antecedents highlight the political rationality of governmentality: the appeal to national security (*raison d'état*) of 16th- and 17th-century European states and the 18th-century liberal economic theories of the Physiocrats and of Adam Smith.

The 1978–9 lectures, *The Birth of Bioethics*, continue the genealogy of governmentality. The titular topic of bioethics is scarcely mentioned, and, toward the end, Foucault apologizes for not getting around to it. Unfortunately, he never returned to the topic, although he had discussed it earlier in HS. The main concern of the lectures is new versions of liberal thought (neo-liberalism) developed in the 20th century: the German Freiburg School of economists who provided the intellectual basis for West Germany's free-market governments following World War II; the French economists who played a similar role for Giscard d'Estaing's government in the 1970s; and the Chicago School (especially Gary Becker), which inspired conservative governments in Great Britain and the United States.

Foucault had a special interest in the Chicago School. Becker and his colleagues reduced governmentality to a minimum, claiming that no plan for the welfare of a population can produce results as good as those produced by the free operation of capitalist markets. But the School allowed considerable disciplinary control (through courts and prisons) of crimes against persons and property. This form of governmentality is still dominant in the United States, with its ironic combination of free markets and mass incarceration.

As he delivered these lectures (in early 1979), Foucault was prescient in thinking that neoliberalism, with its idealized theory of individuals acting entirely from their rational self-interest (*homo economicus*) and of the market as the sole source and criterion of a population's welfare, would become the 'truth of the age'. Foucault, however, was not endorsing neoliberalism as the final truth. He was just recognizing his present moment—which may well extend to today's world—as one in which there is no politically viable alternative (say, Marxist or socialist) to free-market capitalism. Presumably, if Foucault had had time to pursue further his analysis of contemporary governmentality, he would have at least tried to provide tools for constructing meaningful alternatives.

The next three years of lectures turn to the topic of subjectivity. Foucault insists this must be added to his treatments of knowledge and power to complete his overall project, which he now understands as the 'history of truth'. Roughly, his idea is that he has all along been writing histories of how human subjects seek truth by constructing systems of knowledge in a world of power. As we noted in Chapter 4, Foucault had never denied a role for subjectivity, although he cautioned against naive understandings of it. But beginning with his research for his history of sexuality, he took it up as a central theme. In *The Government of the Living* (1979–80), he begins with subjectivity in ancient Greece, returning to the *Oedipus Tyrannus* with reflections on first-person expressions in the play. But for most of the series he turns to baptism, confession, and priestly spiritual guidance as examples of Christian practices designed to lead believers to truth. As we will see, this theme connects to HS IV (*Les aveux de la chair*), but in the following two lecture series, *Subjectivity and Truth* (1980–1) and *The Hermeneutics of the Subject* (1981–2), he returns to the ancients, developing material on the Greeks (for HS II) and on the Romans (HS III).

The last two lecture series, *The Government of Self and Others* (1982–3) and *The Courage of Truth* (1983–4), discuss subjectivity in terms of the ancient Greek philosophical concept of *parrhesia* (truth-telling). *The Government of Self and Others* studies *parrhesia* in political life, as a matter of 'speaking truth to power', for example, when an adviser tells a king that his declaration of war is a mistake or when journalists expose corruption in government. The focus is first on Euripides' *Ion* and Thucydides' discussion of Pericles. But Foucault begins and ends by connecting *parrhesia* to the philosophical way of life. He first thinks through the notion of critique in Kant's 'What Is Enlightenment?', an essay to which he often returned and which he said was something of a 'fetish' for him. The lecture ends with a meta-reflection exploring the idea of taking modern philosophy as a way of life devoted to something like *parrhesia*—an apparently bizarre line of thought but one that becomes more plausible when we think of the lives of, say, Descartes, Spinoza, and Kant. *The Courage of Truth* continues the discussion of *parrhesia* in philosophical life, now returning to the ancient Greeks. Foucault first focuses on Socrates in the *Apology*, 'speaking truth' to the Athenian assembly about his life as a philosopher, and in *Laches* (a dialogue on courage). He concludes with detailed discussions of the Cynics (for example, Antisthenes, Diogenes), who were outspoken critics of established authorities and customs.

Foucault

After Foucault's death, there were hints and rumours that he had completed a fourth volume of his *History of Sexuality*, entitled *The Confessions of the Flesh* (CF), dealing with the Christian Middle Ages. It turns out that Foucault had submitted a typescript of this book to his publisher, Gallimard, in 1982, but in early 1984 recalled it to make final revisions that he never completed. This would seem a paradigm example of what Foucault had in mind when he insisted on 'no posthumous publications'. In 2018, however, the heirs authorized publication of CF, because, as the editor Frédérich Gros drily puts it, 'The heirs of Michel Foucault judged that the time and the circumstances had come to publish this major unpublished work'. The volume is based on the typescript Foucault submitted to Gallimard in 1982. But the editor supplemented the typescript with material from Foucault's handwritten manuscript and added missing section headings. He also included four 'Annexes' (appendices) totalling about forty pages of passages presumably intended for the book but with no clear indication of where they should go. Although the published volume is not quite a finished product, it effectively gives us the next step in Foucault's history of sexuality, moving on from the pagan authors of late antiquity to the Christian fathers, from Clement of Alexandria in the 2nd century AD through Augustine in the 4th and 5th centuries.

Foucault's overall project is to show how these thinkers transferred the core of pagan rules for sexual behaviour into the context of a developing theology of Christian revelation. Here the key—and transforming—factor is the Christian claim that the goal of human life is not any sort of happiness in this world but eternal happiness in a new heavenly life. Of course, theological teachings about sin (for example, the Fall, original sin, forgiveness through baptism and confession) obviously raise the stakes for those guilty of fornication, adultery, and homosexual behaviour; but there is no doubt that such actions merit eternal damnation. There are, however, thorny issues about the salvific significance of the two forms of a chaste life: the virginity that eschews all sexual relations and the marriage that allows sex but only between couples with lifetime commitments to one another. Virginity is no doubt the preferred choice, for those few who can manage it. But does that mean even sex in marriage is sinful or at best an evil tolerated so the human race won't die out? And, if virginity is the ideal, why does Scripture insist on speaking of both virgins and the Church itself as 'brides of Christ'? The bulk of CF consists of close textual analyses of Christian treatises on virginity and on marriage.

As we have seen, Foucault in Volumes II and III developed his accounts of pagan Greek and Roman sexuality in contrast to what he presents as an essentially negative Christian view of sex as such. In Volume IV he presents this view as a much later medieval development (12th century and beyond) and acknowledges that early Christian thinkers—especially Augustine—insist on the intrinsic goodness of sex as a creation of God. At the same time, they recognize the moral dangers of the 'concupiscence' (desire or libido) that is the residue, even after baptism, of original sin. In tracing the early fathers' ideas about the nature of the struggle against the dangers of concupiscence, Foucault finds the origin of the two prime aspects of modern sexuality: the human being as a desiring agent, and the need for continual scrutiny and verbal articulation ('confessions') of the complexities of our sexuality.

CF does not, however, bridge the gap between ancient sexuality and the modern sexuality (from the 16th century on) that was the target of the project Foucault introduced in HS. There still remains a millennium during which Christianity became a Church dominating both secular and religious life and developed the concepts and practices (guilt, self-examination, confession) that lead to the modern desiring self. Part of that period is no doubt covered in an unfinished manuscript *La chair et le corps* (*The Flesh and the Body*), which may well eventually be published. But it's by no means clear that Foucault, had he lived, would have bridged the gap between ancient sexuality and the project sketched in HS on modern sexuality. As the Collège de France lectures show, his research on sexuality was becoming complexly intertwined with studies of subjectivity, governmentality, and truth. To our great loss, we will never see the new horizons a Foucault who lived even a few more years would have brought into view.

References and further reading

Introductions

For an introductory overview, see my articles on Foucault in Edward Craig (ed.), *Routledge Encyclopedia of Philosophy* (New York: Routledge, 1998) and (with Johanna Oksala) Edward Zalta (ed.), *Stanford Encyclopedia of Philosophy* (web-based: <http://plato.stanford.edu/>). For book-length treatments, see Todd May, *Philosophy of Foucault* (Toronto: McGill-Queens University Press, 2006); and Johanna Oskala, *How to Read Foucault* (London: Granta, 2012).

Helpful collections of articles

David Hoy (ed.), *Foucault: A Critical Reader* (Oxford: Blackwell, 1986); Gary Gutting (ed.), *The Cambridge Companion to Foucault*, 2nd edn (Cambridge: Cambridge University Press, 2005); Christopher Falzon et al. (eds), *A Companion to Foucault* (Oxford: Blackwell, 2013); and Diane Taylor, *Michel Foucault: Key Concepts* (London: Routledge, 2014). For some mostly French perspectives on Foucault, see Arnold Davidson (ed.), *Foucault and his Interlocutors* (Chicago: University of Chicago Press, 1997).

Some important monographs

Hubert Dreyfus and Paul Rabinow, *Michel Foucault: Beyond Structuralism and Hermeneutics*, 2nd edn (Chicago: University of Chicago Press, 1983).

Gary Gutting, *Michel Foucault's Archaeology of Scientific Reason* (Cambridge: Cambridge University Press, 1989).

Colin Koopman, *Genealogy as Critique: Foucault and the Problems of Modernity* (Stanford, Calif.: Stanford University Press, 2013).

Lois McNay, *Foucault: A Critical Introduction* (New York: Continuum, 1994).

Ladelle McWhorter, *Bodies and Pleasures: Foucault and the Politics of Sexual Normalization*, Bloomington, Ind.: Indiana University Press, 1999.

Todd May, *Between Genealogy and Epistemology: Psychology, Politics, and Knowledge in the Thought of Michel Foucault* (University Park, Pa.: Pennsylvania State University Press, 1993).

Johanna Oksala, *Foucault on Freedom* (Cambridge: Cambridge University Press, 2005).

John Rajchman, *Michel Foucault: The Freedom of Philosophy* (New York: Columbia University Press, 1985).

Paul Veyne, *Foucault: His Thought, His Character* (Cambridge: Polity, 2010).

Chapter 1: Lives and works

There are three full-length biographies of Foucault: Didier Eribon, *Michel Foucault*, tr. Betsy Wing (Cambridge, Mass.: Harvard University Press, 1991); James Miller, *The Passions of Michel Foucault* (New York: Simon and Schuster, 1993); and David Macey, *The Lives of Michel Foucault* (New York: Pantheon, 1993).

The two striking titles mentioned (and well worth reading beyond the titles) are Patricia Duncker, *Hallucinating Foucault* (Hopewell, NJ: Ecco Press, 1996; reissued, New York: Vintage, 1998) and Maurice Blanchot, 'Foucault as I Imagine Him', translated with Foucault's essay on Blanchot, 'The Thought from Outside', in *Foucault as I Imagine Him and the Thought from Outside*, tr. Jeffrey Mehlman and Brian Massumi (New York and London: MIT Press, 1987).

For a good introduction to Raymond Roussel's life and work, see Mark Ford, *Raymond Roussel and the Republic of Dreams* (Ithaca, NY: Cornell University Press, 2000). Among translations of Raymond Roussel into English, see Trevor Winkfield (ed.), *'How I Wrote Certain of My Books' and Other Writings*, introduction by John Ashbery (Boston: Exact Change, 1995) and *Locus Solus*, tr. Rupert

Copeland Cunningham (Berkeley: University of California Press, 1970).

Foucault nicely expresses the idea of his work as a toolbox in the following comments in a 1974 interview about his expectations for *Discipline and Punish*:

> I want my books to be a sort of toolbox that people can rummage through to find a tool they can use however they want in their own domain...I want the little book that I plan to write on disciplinary systems to be of use for teachers, wardens, magistrates, conscientious objectors. I don't write for an audience, I write for users, not readers.

> ('Prisons et asiles dans le mécanisme du pouvoir',
> DE II, 523–4, my translation)

'Truth, Power, Self', an interview with Foucault, appears in L. H. Martin et al. (eds), *Technologies of the Self: A Seminar with Michel Foucault* (Amherst, Mass.: University of Massachusetts Press, 1988).

Chapter 2: Literature

Bataille's best-known novel (and a focus of Foucault's 'Preface to Transgression') is *The Story of the Eye*, tr. Joachim Neugroschel (San Francisco: City Lights, 1987). For a selection of Bataille's other writings (essays and fiction), see Fred Botting and Scott Wilson (eds), *The Bataille Reader* (Oxford: Blackwell, 1997). Also see Michel Surya, *Georges Bataille: An Intellectual Biography*, tr. Krzysztof Kijalkowski and Michael Richardson (London: Verso, 2002).

For a selection of Blanchot's writings, see Michael Holland (ed.), *The Blanchot Reader* (Oxford: Blackwell, 1995). For a perceptive discussion of Blanchot, see Gerald Bruns, *Maurice Blanchot: The Refusal of Philosophy* (Baltimore and London: Johns Hopkins University Press, 1997).

Georges Perec's famous e-less novel, *La disparition* (1969), has appeared in English as *A Void*, tr. Gilbert Adair (London: The Harvill Press, 1994). For more on the Oulipo movement, see

Warren Motte (ed.), *Oulipo: A Primer of Potential Literature* (Normal, Ill.: Dalkey Archive Press, 1998).

Samuel Beckett's *The Unnamable* is part of a trilogy of novels available in his own translation from the original French as *Three Novels by Samuel Beckett: Molloy, Malone Dies, and the Unnamable* (New York: Grove Press, 1995).

For a good general discussion of Foucault's relation to literary modernism, see Gerald Bruns, 'Foucault's Modernism', in Gary Gutting (ed.), *The Cambridge Companion to Foucault*, 2nd edn (Cambridge: Cambridge University Press, 2005).

Chapter 3: Politics

The references for the passages from Sartre are: *Critique of Dialectical Reason*, Volume I, tr. Alan Sheridan (London: New Left Books, 1976); and two collections of essays, *Between Existentialism and Marxism*, tr. John Mathews (New York: Pantheon, 1983) and *Situations*, tr. Benita Eisler (New York: Braziller, 1965). The *Critique* is Sartre's massive and obscure effort to synthesize existentialism and Marxism; the two collections are more accessible, and could serve as a good introduction to Sartre's thought. On Sartre and Foucault, see Thomas Flynn, *Sartre, Foucault and Historical Reason*, 2 vols (Chicago: University of Chicago Press, 1997, 2005).

Foucault's introduction to Binswanger's essay is available in English (along with that essay) as *Dream and Existence*, tr. Jacob Needleman (New York: Humanities Press, 1986).

Foucault's first book, *Maladie mentale et personnalité* (Paris: Presses Universitaires de France, 1954), was later revised (eliminating the Marxism) and published as *Maladie mentale et psychologie*, translated by Alan Sheridan as *Mental Illness and Psychology* (Berkeley: University of California Press, 1987). Foucault in effect disavowed these early publications; and, in accord with his wishes, neither version was included in the otherwise comprehensive Pléiade collection (*Œuvres*, 2015) of his works.

The Marxist book on punishment that Foucault mentions in *Discipline and Punish* is Georg Rusche and Otto Kirchheimer, *Punishment and Social Structure* (New York: Columbia University Press, 1939).

For Richard Rorty on Foucault, see 'Foucault and Epistemology', in
    David Hoy (ed.), *Foucault: A Critical Reader* (Oxford: Blackwell,
    1986); and 'Foucault/Dewey/Nietzsche', in Richard Rorty, *Essays*
    on Heidegger and Others (Cambridge: Cambridge University Press,
    1991).

Chapter 4: Archaeology

On the *Annales* school of historiography, see Peter Burke, *The French*
    Historical Revolution: The Annales School, 1929-2014 (Palo Alto,
    Calif.: Stanford University Press, 1991) and François Dosse, *New*
    History in France: The Triumph of the Annales, tr. Peter V. Conroy,
    Jr (Urbana, Ill.: University of Illinois Press, 1994).
Andrew Scull's critical comments about *The History of Madness* occur
    in his article 'Michel Foucault's History of Madness', *History of the*
    Human Sciences, 3 (1990), 57.
For Roy Porter's critique of Foucault's work on madness, see
    'Foucault's Great Confinement', *History of the Human Sciences*, 3
    (1990), 47-54. For a discussion of historians' critiques of Foucault
    on madness, see Gary Gutting, 'Foucault and the History of
    Madness', in Gary Gutting (ed.), *The Cambridge Companion to*
    Foucault, 2nd edn (Cambridge: Cambridge University Press,
    2005). For a good collection of essays on Foucault as a historian,
    see Jan Goldstein (ed.), *Foucault and the Writing of History*
    (Cambridge: Blackwell, 1994). Foucault's friend and colleague,
    the Roman historian Paul Veyne, offers a strong appreciation of
    Foucault's historical work in 'Foucault Revolutionizes History', in
    Arnold Davidson (ed.), *Foucault and his Interlocutors* (Chicago:
    University of Chicago Press, 1997).

Chapter 5: Genealogy

Nietzsche's *Genealogy of Morality* is available in an excellent English
    translation with good explanatory notes by Maudemarie Clark and
    Alan Swensen (Indianapolis: Hackett Publishing, 1998). For a
    good commentary on the *Genealogy*, see Brian Leiter, *Nietzsche on*
    Morality (New York: Routledge, 2002).
'Critical Theory/Intellectual History' is an interview with Foucault,
    available in PPC.

Chapter 6: The masked philosopher

For an interesting but controversial interpretation of Foucault as a critical philosopher in the Kantian tradition, see Béatrice Han, *Foucault's Critical Project: Between the Transcendental and the Historical* (Stanford, Calif.: Stanford University Press, 2003).

On Foucault and phenomenology, see Todd May, 'Foucault's Relation to Phenomenology', in Gary Gutting (ed.), *The Cambridge Companion to Foucault*, 2nd edn (Cambridge: Cambridge University Press, 2005).

For more on Foucault's relation to Bachelard and Canguilhem, see Gary Gutting, *Michel Foucault's Archaeology of Scientific Reason* (Cambridge: Cambridge University Press, 1989), chapter 1.

On Foucault and Heidegger, see Hubert Dreyfus, 'Being and Power: Heidegger and Foucault', *International Journal of Philosophical Studies*, 4 (1996), 1–16.

On Sartre versus Heidegger on humanism, see J.-P. Sartre, 'Existentialism is a Humanism', in Walter Kaufmann (ed.), *Existentialism from Dostoyevski to Sartre* (New York: Meridian, 1984) and Martin Heidegger, 'Letter on Humanism', in *Basic Writings* (New York: Harper and Row, 1977).

Chapter 7: Madness

On historians' reactions to Foucault's work on madness, see the references to Chapter 4 above.

Derrida criticizes Foucault's treatment of Descartes on madness in 'Cogito and the History of Madness', *Writing and Difference*, tr. Alan Bass (Chicago: University of Chicago Press, 1978). Foucault responds in 'My Body, This Paper, This Fire', tr. G. P. Bennington, *Oxford Literary Review*, 4 (1979), 5–28.

For a good introduction to the Enlightenment, see Peter Gay, *The Enlightenment: The Rise of Modern Paganism*, new edn (New York: Norton, 1995). For Horkheimer and Adorno's critique of the Enlightenment, see their *Dialectic of Enlightenment*, tr. John Cummings (New York: Continuum, 1976). For a magisterial survey, see Jonathan Israel's trilogy: *Radical Enlightenment, Enlightenment Contested, Democratic Enlightenment* (Oxford: Oxford University Press, 2002, 2009, 2013).

Regarding Foucault and Canguilhem on experience, see Gary Gutting, 'Foucault's Philosophy of Experience', *Boundary 2*, 29 (2002), 69–86.

Chapter 8: Crime and punishment

For a good general discussion of Foucault on power and knowledge, see Joseph Rouse, 'Power/Knowledge', in Gary Gutting (ed.), *The Cambridge Companion to Foucault*, 2nd edn (Cambridge: Cambridge University Press, 2005).

For an excellent analysis and critique of Foucault as a theoretician (rather than a historian) of power, see Axel Honneth, *The Critique of Power: Reflective Stages in Critical Social Theory* (Boston: MIT Press, 1991).

Chapter 9: Modern sex

On Foucault and gay issues, see David Halperin, *Saint Foucault: Towards a Gay Hagiography* (New York: Oxford University Press, 1995).

In presenting the Jouy case, I have referred both to HS and to Foucault's more extensive discussion in the Collège de France lecture series, *Abnormal*. For Linda Alcoff's critique, see 'Dangerous Pleasures: Foucault and the Politics of Pedophilia', in Susan Hekman (ed.), *Feminist Interpretations of Foucault* (University Park, Pa.: Pennsylvania State Press, 1996). Jana Sawicki generally supports Alcoff in her review of *Abnormal* for *Notre Dame Philosophical Reviews* (2005.01.03). Shelley Tremain's respose to Alcoff and Jawicki, is in 'Educating Jouy', *Hypatia*, 10 (2013).

On Herculine Barbin, see Michel Foucault (ed.), *Herculine Barbin: Being the Recently Discovered Memoirs of a Nineteenth-Century Hermaphrodite*, tr. R. McDougall (New York: Pantheon, 1975).

For some interesting work on the history of sexuality in a Foucaultian manner, see Arnold Davidson, *The Emergence of Sexuality: Historical Epistemology and the Formation of Concepts* (Cambridge, Mass.: Harvard University Press, 2001).

Chapter 10: Ancient sex

For Pierre Hadot on (especially ancient) philosophy, see his *What Is Ancient Philosophy?*, tr. Michael Chase (Cambridge, Mass.: Harvard University Press, 2002) and *Philosophy as a Way of Life: Spiritual Exercises from Socrates to Foucault*, ed. Arnold Davidson, tr. Michael Chase (Oxford: Blackwell, 1995).

For reactions of classicists to Foucault's work on ancient sexuality, see
David H. J. Larmour et al. (eds), *Rethinking Sexuality: Foucault
and Classical Antiquity* (Princeton: Princeton University
Press, 1997).

Chapter 11: Foucault after Foucault

The website for Columbia University's 2015–16 seminar, *Foucault
13/13*, directed by Bernard Harcourt, offers very helpful analyses
and discussions of each of the thirteen year-long lectures: <http://
blogs.law.columbia.edu/foucault1313/>. See also Stuart Elden,
Foucault's Last Decade (Cambridge: Polity, 2016), which provides
excellent background to the Collège de France lectures as well as
to Foucault's other lectures and writings from his last ten years.

For details on the posthumous publications, see Stuart Elden's review
of *Les aveux de la chair*, 'Foucault's Confessions of the Flesh',
Theory, Culture & Society, 28 March 2018 (<https://www.
theoryculturesociety.org/review-foucaults-confessions-flesh/>).

Foucault's 'lot of rubbish' comment was made in conversation with his
editor, Pierre Nora, as reported by Stuart Elden in *Foucault's Last
Decade*.

The passage from Dumézil is as cited by Bernard Harcourt, *Foucault
13/13*, introduction to Seminar 1.

On governmentality, see Graham Burchell et al. (eds), *The Foucault
Effect: Studies in Governmentality* (Chicago: University of Chicago
Press, 1991), which includes two essays by and an interview with
Foucault; also Johanna Oksala's excellent *Foucault, Politics, and
Violence* (Evanston, Ill.: Northwestern University Press, 2012).

On Foucault's view of subjectivity, see Laura Cremonesi et al. (eds),
Foucault and the Making of Subjects (London: Rowman and
Littlefield, 2016).

For a discussion of Foucault's late work on *parrhesia* and philosophy
as a way of life (and its relation to his earlier work), see Edward
McGushkin, *Foucault's* Askesis: *An Introduction to the
Philosophical Life* (Evanston, Ill.: Northwestern University Press,
2007).

Index

Index

THE AMERICAN PRESIDENCY

A Very Short Introduction

Charles O. Jones

This marvellously concise survey is packed with information about the presidency, some of it quite surprising. We learn, for example, that the Founders adopted the word "president" over "governor" and other alternatives because it suggested a light hand, as in one who presides, rather than rules. Indeed, the Constitutional Convention first agreed to a weak chief executive elected by congress for one seven-year term, later calling for independent election and separation of powers. Jones sheds much light on how assertive leaders, such as Andrew Jackson, Theodore Roosevelt, and FDR enhanced the power of the presidency, and illuminating how such factors as philosophy (Reagan's anti-Communist conservatism), the legacy of previous presidencies (Jimmy Carter following Watergate), relations with Congress, and the impact of outside events have all influenced presidential authority.

> "In this brief but timely book, a leading expert takes us back to the creation of the presidency and insightfully explains the challenges of executive leadership in a separated powers system."
>
> George C. Edwards III, Distinguished Professor of Political Science, Texas A&M University

KEYNES
A Very Short Introduction
Robert Skidelsky

John Maynard Keynes (1883–1946) is a central thinker of the twentieth century, not just an economic theorist and statesman, but also in economics, philosophy, politics, and culture. In this *Very Short Introduction* Lord Skidelsky, a renowned biographer of Keynes, explores his ethical and practical philosophy, his monetary thought, and provides an insight into his life and works. In the recent financial crisis Keynes's theories have become more timely than ever, and remain at the centre of political and economic discussion. With a look at his major works and his contribution to twentieth-century economic thought, Skidelsky considers Keynes's legacy on today's society.

HUMAN RIGHTS
A Very Short Introduction
Andrew Clapham

An appeal to human rights in the face of injustice can be a heartfelt and morally justified demand for some, while for others it remains merely an empty slogan. Taking an international perspective and focusing on highly topical issues such as torture, arbitrary detention, privacy, health and discrimination, this *Very Short Introduction* will help readers to understand for themselves the controversies and complexities behind this vitally relevant issue. Looking at the philosophical justification for rights, the historical origins of human rights and how they are formed in law, Andrew Clapham explains what our human rights actually are, what they might be, and where the human rights movement is heading.

www.oup.com/vsi

GERMAN PHILOSOPHY
A Very Short Introduction
Andrew Bowie

German Philosophy: A Very Short Introduction discusses the idea that German philosophy forms one of the most revealing responses to the problems of 'modernity'. The rise of the modern natural sciences and the related decline of religion raises a series of questions, which recur throughout German philosophy, concerning the relationships between knowledge and faith, reason and emotion, and scientific, ethical, and artistic ways of seeing the world. There are also many significant philosophers who are generally neglected in most existing English-language treatments of German philosophy, which tend to concentrate on the canonical figures. This *Very Short Introduction* will include reference to these thinkers and suggests how they can be used to question more familiar German philosophical thought.